BASIC II
Advanced

BASIC II
Advanced

WILLIAM C. CONLEY

University of Wisconsin–Green Bay

PBI
a petrocelli
book
new york / princeton

Copyright © 1983 Petrocelli Books, Inc.
All rights reserved.

Designed by Diane L. Backes
Typesetting by Backes Graphics

Printed in the United States of America
1 2 3 4 5 6 7 8 9 10

Library of Congress Cataloging in Publication Data

Conley, William C., 1948–
  BASIC II Advanced.

  Includes index.
  1. BASIC (Computer program language) I. Title.
QA76.73.B3C656   1983   001.64'24   83-12089
ISBN 0-89433-202-3

To

the Yuncks—
John, Ruth, Tom, and Ed

Table of Contents

Introduction

PART ONE

Advanced Problems

PART TWO

Futuristic Problems

Introduction

The author suggests that *BASIC for Beginners* be read before attempting this volume. However, for those readers who want to start with this text, a short review of BASIC, summation notation, and integral calculus is given in chapter 1.

PART I

Advanced Problems

Brief Review 1

Many times in mathematics, statistics, business and science it is necessary to add things up. To facilitate this, the sigma notation (Σ) has been developed. If you want the sum of the fourteen variables, $X_1, X_2, X_3, X_4, X_5, X_6, X_7, X_8, X_9, X_{10}, X_{11}, X_{12}, X_{13}, X_{14}$, you can write them as $X_1 + X_2 + X_3 + X_4 + X_5 + X_6 + X_7 + X_8 + X_9 + X_{10} + X_{11} + X_{12} + X_{13} + X_{14}$. Using the Σ instead of the previous sum, we write

$$\sum_{i=1}^{14} X_i$$

which means that as the subscript i goes from 1 to 2 to 3, ..., 14, the fourteen variables are summed. Therefore,

$$\sum_{i=1}^{100} X_i^2$$

means $X_1^2 + X_2^2 + X_3^2 + \ldots + X_{100}^2$, saving much space.

Also double, triple or quadruple sums are possible. For example,

$$\sum_{i=1}^{5} \sum_{j=1}^{4} X_{ij}$$

3

would mean the sum over all i's and j's of X_{ij}, or in this case

$$X_{11} + X_{12} + X_{13} + X_{14}$$
$$+ X_{21} + X_{22} + X_{23} + X_{24}$$
$$+ X_{31} + X_{32} + X_{33} + X_{34}$$
$$+ X_{41} + X_{42} + X_{43} + X_{44}$$
$$+ X_{51} + X_{52} + X_{53} + X_{54}$$

In this case i might represent the row and j the column. So X_{43} might be the entry in the 4th row and 3rd column.

_____REVIEW OF BASIC

A computer program in BASIC consists of a series of statements written vertically on a page, and operated on by the computer sequentially from the top to the bottom in order, unless the order of flow is interrupted by a direct or conditional command.

But what does this mean? Before looking at some examples, there are a few rules of BASIC. All statements are numbered to keep track of them. BASIC uses variables, or letters, like $A, B, C, D, \ldots, X, Y, Z$ to keep track of things. Numbers can be assigned to letters. The PRINT command tells the computer to print out information; the READ command tells it to accept input information (data). STOP and END are used at the end of the program; + means add, – means subtract or minus, / means divide, * means multiply and ** means raise to a power or exponentiation. In BASIC, = means equals, but in a right to left sense. For example, in BASIC X=3.8 assigns the number 3.8 to the variable or letter X. The number must be on the right and the variable on the left. An expression such as X=3.8*Y+2*Z is also acceptable provided that *Y* and *Z* have been assigned numerical values in previous statements.

Now let's write a complete program in BASIC to calculate and print out the values of $Y = X + 5$ for X = 1, 2, 3, 4, 5, 6, 7, 8, 9 and 10. The program is:

```
8   FOR X=1 TO 10
20  Y=X+5
30  PRINT X,Y
40  NEXT X
50  STOP
60  END
```

The printout is:

```
 1  6
 2  7
 3  8
 4  9
 5  10
 6  11
 7  12
 8  13
 9  14
10  15
```

The *FOR NEXT* statement sequence is the most powerful and useful command in BASIC. In this case 8 FOR X=1 TO 10 tells the computer to go from line 8 to 20 to 30 to 40 with *X* = 1. Then it tells the computer to go back to line 8 and make *X* = 2. Next it tells the computer to go from line 8 to 20 to 30 to 40. Then *X* = 3, and the computer goes from line 8 to 20 to 30 to 40 again. Then *X* = 4, and the computer goes from line 8 to 20 to 30 to 40 again. And it does this six more times with X = 5, 6, 7, 8, 9 and 10. In computer programming this *FOR NEXT* sequence is frequently called a *loop*.

The computer proceeds as follows: In line 8 X is assigned the value 1; the computer then goes to line 20 where the current value of X (namely, 1) is added to 5 to obtain 6. Then 6 is assigned (remember, = means "is assigned right to left") to Y. 30 PRINT X,Y prints the current values of X and Y, or 1 6 in this case. 40 NEXT X sends the computer back to line 8 where X becomes 2, and then 20 Y=X+5 where Y is assigned the current value of X (2 in this case) plus 5, or 7. Then 30 PRINT X,Y prints the current values of X and Y or 2 7. This continues with X and Y becoming 3 8, 4 9, etc., until 10 15 for X and Y.

At this point the *FOR NEXT* loop is satisfied because another increment would make X = 11, and 8 FOR X=1 TO 10 tells the computer to stop the looping when the X = 10 loop is done. At this point the computer goes to the next statement below 40 NEXT X, namely 50 STOP and 60 END. This ends the program. (Some computers require only the END statement, not STOP and END together, to end the program.)

Now certainly the reader could have added 5 to the numbers 1 through 10 and written down the results. So why have a computer? First of all, the computer does the calculation many times faster; therefore, in more complicated and longer problems the computer would be helpful. Also, the computer never makes mistakes. It always does exactly what a human tells it to do. Thus, the secret to programming is to be detailed and careful enough so that what you tell the computer to do is exactly what you want it to do. In other words, as with English, we must communicate in BASIC clearly and effectively.

There are a few more rules of BASIC we should learn, but let's write another program first. Write a BASIC program to find the sum (total) of all the counting numbers from 1 to 250.

In other words, we want to total $1 + 2 + 3 + 4 + 5 + 6 + \ldots$ + 250. The BASIC program to do this is:

```
5    S=0
10   FOR X=1 TO 250
15   S=S+X
20   NEXT X
25   PRINT S
30   STOP
35   END
```

The printout is:

31375.

So 31,375 is the sum of all the counting numbers from 1 to 250, and of course the program ran in a fraction of a second. Let's go over the program. Line 5 initializes (sets up) the variable S to be zero. Line 10 FOR X=1 TO 250, starts the *FOR NEXT* sequence that will loop 250 times through lines 10, 15 and 20. Line 15 S=S+X does the addition on the right-hand side of the equals sign and assigns this sum to the variable S on the left-hand side. The first time through $X = 1$, so $S + X$ is $0 + 1$, and $S = 1$ is the result (S leaves line 15 with the value 1). Then 20 NEXT X sends the computer back to line 10 where X is increased to 2. Then $S = S + X$ is $S = 1 + 2$, so $S = 3$ when it leaves line 15 the second time. Again 20 NEXT X leads back to line 10 where X is increased to 3. Then 15 S=S+X. S is the old value of S, or 3, plus the new value of X, or 3; thus $3 + 3 = 6$ on the right-hand side and this sum (6) is assigned to S on the left. Then *NEXT X*, and $X = 4$, and that is added so that $S = 10$, and so on until $X = 250$ is added the 250th time through the loop. Then 25 PRINT S prints the current value of S which at this point (the end of the program) is 31,375.

Notice that this time the PRINT statement was outside the loop, since we just wanted the final total of $1 + 2 + 3 + 4 + \ldots + 250$ (all 250 numbers). In the first program we wanted the value of $Y = X + 5$ for each X so we put the print statement inside the *FOR NEXT* loop. It depends on what kind of problem you are trying to solve as to where the PRINT statement should go.

One other point—always use capital letters in writing BASIC programs. Small letters do not make the program wrong (it is the logic that counts), but programs are entered into the computer by keypunched cards or teletype terminals (called computer terminals), and these machines only type in capitals. Thus, printed capital letters have become a standard convention in BASIC. This is also true in other computer languages like FORTRAN and COBOL.

Let's try another example. Write a BASIC program to find the sum of the even counting numbers from 2 through 100 individually raised to the fourth power. We want $2 \cdot 2 \cdot 2 \cdot 2 + 4 \cdot 4 \cdot 4 \cdot 4 + 6 \cdot 6 \cdot 6 \cdot 6 + 8 \cdot 8 \cdot 8 \cdot 8 + \ldots + 100 \cdot 100 \cdot 100 \cdot 100$, or in shorthand exponential notation $2^4 + 4^4 + 6^4 + 8^4 + \ldots + 100^4$ (the sum of all 50 terms). The program is:

```
 5   S=0
10   FOR X=2 TO 100 STEP 2
15   S=S+X**4
20   NEXT X
25   PRINT S
30   STOP
35   END
```

The printout is:

$$1.05067 \text{ E}09$$

E09 means 1 x 10^9 or move the decimal over nine places to the right. So the number is really 1,050,670,000 in this case. Notice that this program is similar to the previous program except that 10 FOR X=2 TO 100 STEP 2 tells the computer that the lines 10, 15 and 20 will be executed 50 times with $X = 2$ the first time, $X = 4$ the second time, $X = 6$ the third time, $X = 8$ the fourth time and $X = 100$ the fiftieth time. STEP 2 makes the X increment by 2 each time (in the absence of the STEP increment, the X variable is increased by one each time as before).

The line 15 S=S+X**4 adds a new term each time through as in the previous program, except this time the increment is the current value of X multiplied by itself four times (**4 accomplishes this in BASIC).

Now let's learn a few more rules and features of BASIC. Sometimes business or science problems require that data be read in a way that does not follow a pattern like 1, 2, 3, 4, ... In these cases the READ and DATA statements are used. Let's introduce these statements by writing a BASIC program to read in and add up the numbers 81, 62, 53.8, 25, 143.6, 52.1, 19.3, 21, 5 and 4. The program is:

```
5    S=0
12   FOR I=1 TO 10
15   READ X
20   S=S+X
30   NEXT I
40   PRINT S
50   DATA 81, 62, 53.8, 25, 143.6
60   DATA 52.1, 19.3, 21, 5, 4
70   STOP
80   END
```

The printout of the total (*S*) is:

466.8.

Again *S* is initialized to zero to get the summation started correctly. 12 FOR I=1 TO 10 tells the computer to go from statement 12 to 15 to 20 to 30 ten times, for the ten numbers that must be summed. This time the variable *I* is just used as a counter and does not figure in the calculation at all. 15 READ X tells the computer to take the piece of data (81) on the left end of the first data statement and assign it to *X*. Then 20 S=S+X makes *S* = 0 + 81. Thus, *S* is 81. 30 NEXT I sends the computer back to 12, and then at 15 READ X the computer takes the next data point (62) and assigns it to *X*. Then 20 S=S+X makes *S* = 81 + 62, or 143. And so on reading data left to right (81, 62, 53.8, 25, 143.6, 52.1, 19.3, 21, 5, 4 in this order) top to bottom and summing it. When the *FOR NEXT* loop is completely satisfied (ten times through in this case), then 40 PRINT S prints the current value of *S*, which at this point is 466.8, the total.

DATA statements can be put anywhere in the program, although most programmers put them right before the end of the program. The computer jumps to the DATA statement, takes the next piece of data, and assigns it to whatever variable is in the READ line.

Now for a few more rules. As implied earlier, all BASIC statements must be numbered with whole numbers of increasing size. It is best to have a number scheme of 5, 10, 15, 20, etc. (with jumps in the sequence), so that if a new statement is needed, say, between lines 10 and 15, then 11, 12, 13, or 14 are available for numbering it. This prevents having to renumber all statements.

In BASIC only the letters of the alphabet (*A, B, C, D, E,* . . . , *X, Y, Z*) and letters followed by a single whole number (0, 1, 2, 3, 4, 5, 6, 7, 8, 9) can be used as variables. So the variables are:

$$A \ , B \ , C \ , \ldots , X \ , Y \ , Z$$
$$A0, B0, C0, \ldots , X0, Y0, Z0$$
$$A1, B1, C1, \ldots , X1, Y1, Z1$$
$$A2, B2, C2, \ldots , X2, Y2, Z2$$
$$A3, B3, C3, \ldots , X3, Y3, Z3$$
$$A4, B4, C4, \ldots , X4, Y4, Z4$$
$$A5, B5, C5, \ldots , X5, Y5, Z5$$
$$A6, B6, C6, \ldots , X6, Y6, Z6$$
$$A7, B7, C7, \ldots , X7, Y7, Z7$$
$$A8, B8, C8, \ldots , X8, Y8, Z8$$
$$A9, B9, C9, \ldots , X9, Y9, Z9$$

Below are the symbols used in BASIC and their meanings:

$>$ greater than
$<$ less than
$=$ equal (actually value on right is assigned to variable on left)
$=>$ greater than or equal
$<=$ less than or equal
$><$ not equal
$+$ add
$-$ minus or negative
$/$ divide
$*$ multiply
$**$ raise to a power

"GO TO line number" means go directly to the line number named, for example, GO TO 55 means go directly to the line numbered 55.

IF a THEN s means if a is true then go to line s. However, if a is false, then just go to the next line. Example: IF X>9 THEN 22 means if the current value of X is greater than 9, then go to line 22; however, if $X > 9$ is false, then the computer goes to the next statement. These *IF* statements and series of *IF* statements give the programmer control over sophisticated programs (we will write some in later chapters).

Remember that each BASIC statement is executed by the computer sequentially from top to bottom unless a *FOR NEXT* loop, *IF THEN, GO TO,* or *READ DATA* command orders it to another spot in the program. Within these limitations and rules, you are free to write as practical, useful, creative and spectacular programs as your imagination and understanding will permit. Two programs could look completely different and accomplish exactly the same thing correctly. Never let anyone tell you that your programming style is not good. If it is right for you and your programs work, then it is a good style.

_____EXERCISES

1.1. Write a BASIC program to find the sum of the odd numbers from 1 to 1000 (1, 3, 5, . . . , 999).

1.2. Write a similar program to find the sum of the even numbers from 1 to 1000 (2, 4, 6, . . . , 1000).

1.3. Write a BASIC program to convert 1, 2, 3, 4, 5, 6, 7, 8, 9 and 10 kilometers into miles (1 kilometer equals .62 miles).

1.4. Write a BASIC program to add up the numbers 10, 11, 12, . . . , 100.

1.5. Write a program to calculate how many seconds there are in a year of 365 days.

1.6. Write a program to convert 1 to 500 francs to their dollar equivalents and print out this chart (1 dollar equals 7 francs).

Some Basic Built-In Functions

These functions are preprogrammed into the BASIC language for use as the need arises. They arc uocd (some fairly often) in science and business applications. They are:

Function	*Purpose*
SIN(X)	sine of X
COS(X)	cosine of X
TAN(X)	tangent of X
ATN(X)	arctangent of X
EXP(X)	number e raised to the X power
ABS(X)	absolute value of X
LOG(X)	common logarithm of X
SQR(X)	square root of X
INT(X)	integer (whole number) content of X

____REVIEW OF INTEGRAL CALCULUS

The area under a curve can be treated as an integral (infinite or finite sum) and approximated accurately using BASIC programs. Isaac Newton and Gottfried Leibnitz figured out the theoretical part of this in the seventeenth century and called it calculus. Let's look at an example.

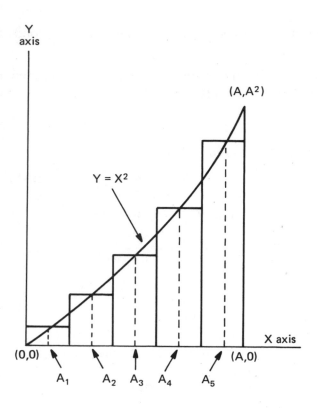

We want the area under the curve $Y = X^2$ from 0 to A. Notice that the five big rectangles approximate it pretty well. In this case the area of the rectangles would be:

$$A_1^2\frac{A}{5} + A_2^2\frac{A}{5} + A_3^2\frac{A}{5} + A_4^2\frac{A}{5} + A_5^2\frac{A}{5}$$

You see that part of each rectangle is too big and part is too small for the curve, so they tend to average out and approximate the area. As more and more tiny rectangles are added to the partition, the approximation gets better and better. This can be called taking the limit, as n goes to infinity.

For practice let's find the area under the curve (called finding the integral) of X^2 from 0 to 20. This is usually written as $\int_0^{20} X^2$, and read "the integral of X^2 from 0 to 20." Let's have there be 2,000 rectangles each of width 20/2,000 or 0.01. The program is:

```
 5   =0
10   FOR I=0 TO 19.99 STEP .01
15   X=I+.005
20   S=S+.01*X**2
30   NEXT I
40   PRINT S
50   STOP
60   END
```

The printout is:

2666.67

I goes from 0 to 19.99 by increments of 0.01 giving us 2,000 rectangles. $X=I+.005$ centers X in the middle of each rectangle. The subsequent $X**2$ represents the height of the rectangle, and 0.01 is the constant width. S just sums the areas of the 2,000 rectangles. The true area is 2,666.6667. Notice how close our approximation with the 2,000 rectangles is.

_____**EXERCISES**

1.7. Find $\int_0^{62} X^2 - \sqrt{X}$.

1.8. Find $\int_0^{30} X^3$.

1.9. Find $\int_{-40}^{40} X^3$.

The Normal Curve 2

Most people have heard of the bell shaped curve or grading on a curve or the normal curve. These are names and expressions for Karl Fredrich Gauss's normal theory of errors and the central limit theorem. The curve was originally called the Gaussian curve after its discoverer. However, today it is usually referred to as simply the normal curve.

It turns out that many events, processes, formulae and theories follow the normal curve. We want to pursue this a bit in the remainder of the text, but as a point of departure, let's assume that the normal curve is very important (which it is) and let's study it and try to produce its "function values." Then we will explain more fully its uses and applications.

The normal curve function is defined to be

$$Z = (1/(\sigma\sqrt{2\pi}))\exp(-.5(X-\mu/\sigma)^2)$$

where σ is the standard deviation (a measure of how spread out the curve is); π is the circumference of a circle divided by its diameter (or approximately 3.141593); exp (or just e) is the base of the natural logarithms; μ is the average value or mean of the distribution; X is the value along the x-axis and

FIGURE 2.1 NORMAL CURVE.

Z is the height along the y-axis (Z is usually used for the normal curve height value).

Each different pair (μ, σ) gives a different normal curve. Some normal curves are short and wide, some are tall and thin. One such example of a normal curve would be in Figure 2.1. The most commonly used normal curve is the one where μ = 0 and σ = 1. (More about the explanation later.) This is the so-called standard normal curve and its function is

$$Z = (1./\sqrt{2\pi})\exp(-.5X^2)$$

This curve is a little shorter and wider than the one in the figure. The area under the curve is one. The curve is completely symmetric about zero. So, for example, the area from 0 to 1.19 is the same as the area from −1.19 to 0, etc.

We need these standard normal area values. So let's write a BASIC integral program to find the areas (probabilities) under the normal curve from 0 to 0.01, from 0 to 0.02 and so on from 0 to 3.00 (by increments of 0.01).

```
1       PRINT "Z", "AREA"
2       T=2*3.141593
3       R-0
4       K=0
5       FOR J=.01 TO 3.00 STEP .01
7       S=0
8       J5=J-.0001
10      FOR I=K TO J5 STEP .0001
15      X=I+.00005
20      S=S+.0001*(1./SQR(T))*EXP(-.5*X**2)
25      NEXT I
30      K=K+.01
35      R=R+S
40      PRINTUSING 42,J,R
42:     #.##        #.####
```

```
45     NEXT J
50     STOP
60     END
RUN
13:38  SEP 11 NORMAL . . .
Z      AREA
 0.01  0.0040
 0.02  0.0080
 0.03  0.0120
 0.04  0.0160
 0.05  0.0199
 0.06  0.0239
 0.07  0.0279
 0.08  0.0319
 0.09  0.0359
 0.10  0.0398
 0.11  0.0438
 0.12  0.0478
 0.13  0.0517
 0.14  0.0557
 0.15  0.0596
 0.16  0.0636
 0.17  0.0675
 0.18  0.0714
 0.19  0.0753
 0.20  0.0793
 0.21  0.0832
 0.22  0.0871
 0.23  0.0910
 0.24  0.0948
 0.25  0.0987
 0.26  0.1026
 0.27  0.1064
 0.28  0.1103
 0.29  0.1141
```

0.30	0.1179
0.31	0.1217
0.32	0.1255
0.33	0.1293
0.34	0.1331
0.35	0.1368
0.36	0.1406
0.37	0.1443
0.38	0.1480
0.39	0.1517
0.40	0.1554
0.41	0.1591
0.42	0.1628
0.43	0.1664
0.44	0.1700
0.45	0.1736
0.46	0.1772
0.47	0.1808
0.48	0.1844
0.49	0.1879
0.50	0.1915
0.51	0.1950
0.52	0.1985
0.53	0.2019
0.54	0.2054
0.55	0.2088
0.56	0.2123
0.57	0.2157
0.58	0.2190
0.59	0.2224
0.60	0.2257
0.61	0.2291
0.62	0.2324
0.63	0.2357
0.64	0.2389

0.65	0.2422
0.66	0.2454
0.67	0.2486
0.68	0.2517
0.69	0.2549
0.70	0.2580
0.71	0.2611
0.72	0.2642
0.73	0.2673
0.74	0.2703
0.75	0.2734
0.76	0.2764
0.77	0.2794
0.78	0.2823
0.79	0.2852
0.80	0.2881
0.81	0.2910
0.82	0.2939
0.83	0.2967
0.84	0.2995
0.85	0.3023
0.86	0.3051
0.87	0.3078
0.88	0.3106
0.89	0.3133
0.90	0.3159
0.91	0.3186
0.92	0.3212
0.93	0.3238
0.94	0.3264
0.95	0.3289
0.96	0.3315
0.97	0.3340
0.98	0.3365
0.99	0.3389

1.00	0.3413
1.01	0.3438
1.02	0.3461
1.03	0.3485
1.04	0.3508
1.05	0.3531
1.06	0.3554
1.07	0.3577
1.08	0.3599
1.09	0.3621
1.10	0.3643
1.11	0.3665
1.12	0.3686
1.13	0.3708
1.14	0.3729
1.15	0.3749
1.16	0.3770
1.17	0.3790
1.18	0.3810
1.19	0.3830
1.20	0.3849
1.21	0.3869
1.22	0.3888
1.23	0.3907
1.24	0.3925
1.25	0.3944
1.26	0.3962
1.27	0.3980
1.28	0.3997
1.29	0.4015
1.30	0.4032
1.31	0.4049
1.32	0.4066
1.33	0.4082
1.34	0.4099

1.35	0.4115
1.36	0.4131
1.37	0.4147
1.38	0.4162
1.39	0.4177
1.40	0.4192
1.41	0.4207
1.42	0.4222
1.43	0.4236
1.44	0.4251
1.45	0.4265
1.46	0.4279
1.47	0.4292
1.48	0.4306
1.49	0.4319
1.50	0.4332
1.51	0.4345
1.52	0.4357
1.53	0.4370
1.54	0.4382
1.55	0.4394
1.56	0.4406
1.57	0.4418
1.58	0.4429
1.59	0.4441
1.60	0.4452
1.61	0.4463
1.62	0.4474
1.63	0.4484
1.64	0.4495
1.65	0.4505
1.66	0.4515
1.67	0.4525
1.68	0.4535
1.69	0.4545

1.70	0.4554
1.71	0.4564
1.72	0.4573
1.73	0.4582
1.74	0.4591
1.75	0.4599
1.76	0.4608
1.77	0.4616
1.78	0.4625
1.79	0.4633
1.80	0.4641
1.81	0.4649
1.82	0.4656
1.83	0.4664
1.84	0.4671
1.85	0.4678
1.86	0.4686
1.87	0.4693
1.88	0.4699
1.89	0.4706
1.90	0.4713
1.91	0.4719
1.92	0.4726
1.93	0.4732
1.94	0.4738
1.95	0.4744
1.96	0.4750
1.97	0.4756
1.98	0.4761
1.99	0.4767
2.00	0.4772
2.01	0.4778
2.02	0.4783
2.03	0.4788
2.04	0.4793

2.05	0.4798
2.06	0.4803
2.07	0.4808
2.08	0.4812
2.09	0.4817
2.10	0.4821
2.11	0.4826
2.12	0.4830
2.13	0.4834
2.14	0.4838
2.15	0.4842
2.16	0.4846
2.17	0.4850
2.18	0.4854
2.19	0.4857
2.20	0.4861
2.21	0.4864
2.22	0.4868
2.23	0.4871
2.24	0.4875
2.25	0.4878
2.26	0.4881
2.27	0.4884
2.28	0.4887
2.29	0.4890
2.30	0.4893
2.31	0.4896
2.32	0.4898
2.33	0.4901
2.34	0.4904
2.35	0.4906
2.36	0.4909
2.37	0.4911
2.38	0.4913
2.39	0.4916

2.40	0.4918
2.41	0.4920
2.42	0.4922
2.43	0.4925
2.44	0.4927
2.45	0.4929
2.46	0.4931
2.47	0.4932
2.48	0.4934
2.49	0.4936
2.50	0.4938
2.51	0.4940
2.52	0.4941
2.53	0.4943
2.54	0.4945
2.55	0.4946
2.56	0.4948
2.57	0.4949
2.58	0.4951
2.59	0.4952
2.60	0.4953
2.61	0.4955
2.62	0.4956
2.63	0.4957
2.64	0.4959
2.65	0.4960
2.66	0.4961
2.67	0.4962
2.68	0.4963
2.69	0.4964
2.70	0.4965
2.71	0.4966
2.72	0.4967
2.73	0.4968
2.74	0.4969

2.75	0.4970
2.76	0.4971
2.77	0.4972
2.78	0.4973
2.79	0.4974
2.80	0.4974
2.81	0.4975
2.82	0.4976
2.83	0.4977
2.84	0.4977
2.85	0.4978
2.86	0.4979
2.87	0.4979
2.88	0.4980
2.89	0.4981
2.90	0.4981
2.91	0.4982
2.92	0.4982
2.93	0.4983
2.94	0.4984
2.95	0.4984
2.96	0.4985
2.97	0.4985
2.98	0.4986
2.99	0.4986
3.00	0.4987

Note: The PRINTUSING statement allows you to control the format of the printing (how many decimal places, etc.) Each # represents a one place holder.

Now that we have these normal curve values, let's look up a few normal curve values and work on some problems.

Statisticians are fond of the statement "the probability of such and such, etc." So they have adopted the symbol $P(\ )$ to mean "the probability that the event in parentheses has occurred." $P(A)$ means the probability that event A has happened, etc. Now Z is the usual symbol for any event, process or formula that is standard normally distributed. Therefore, as an example, what is the probability that a standard normal value is between 0 and 1.39? Or what is $P(0 \leqslant Z \leqslant 1.39)$? We can read it off of the chart we just constructed. The answer is 0.4177. In other words, if you had one million numbers in a hat that were standard normally distributed and selected one at random, you would stand a 41.77% chance of the number being between 0 and 1.39.

Incidentally, because the normal curve is a continuous distribution (any number from $-\infty$ to $+\infty$ can occur):

$$P(0 < Z < 1.39) = P(0 \leqslant Z \leqslant 1.39) = P(0 \leqslant Z < 1.39)$$
$$= P(0 < Z \leqslant 1.39) = 0.4177$$

Let's try a few more. What is $P(0 \leqslant Z \leqslant 2.24)$? From the chart we get 0.4875. $P(1.12 \leqslant Z \leqslant 1.96)$ is $P(0 \leqslant Z \leqslant 1.96)$ $- P(0 \leqslant Z \leqslant 1.12) = 0.4750 - 0.3686 = 0.1064$.

Note that $P(0 \leqslant Z) = 0.5$. Z can go to $+\infty$, but values (areas or probabilities) are rarely calculated beyond 3.00 because there is so little area beyond +3.00. Remember that a similar thing is true for -3.00 and $-\infty$.

What is $P(-1.39 \leqslant Z \leqslant 0)$? It is exactly equal to $P(0 \leqslant Z \leqslant 1.39) = 0.4177$ due to the complete symmetry of the standard normal curve about zero.

What is $P(-2.38 \leqslant Z \leqslant -0.56)$? It is equal to $P(0.56 \leqslant Z \leqslant 2.38) = P(0 \leqslant Z \leqslant 2.38) - P(0 \leqslant Z \leqslant 0.56) = 0.4913 - 0.2123 = 0.2790$.

What is $P(Z \geqslant 1.30)$? It is equal to $0.5 - P(0 \leqslant Z \leqslant 1.30) = 0.5 - 0.4032 = 0.0968$.

What is $P(Z \leqslant -1.91)$? It is $0.5 - P(0 \leqslant Z \leqslant 1.91) = 0.5 - 0.4719 = 0.0281$.

What is $P(-1.83 \leqslant Z \leqslant 2.53)$? It is $P(0 \leqslant Z \leqslant 1.83) + P(0 \leqslant Z \leqslant 2.53) = 0.4664 + 0.4943 = 0.9607$.

This is all very interesting, but does it mean anything? Are there uses for the normal curve? The answer is yes. Let's look at a few more definitions and concepts, and then we will start doing some problems with our standard normal values.

The mean of a set of values is the numerical average. It is usually denoted by the symbol $\overline{X}$ (said "X bar").

$$\overline{X} = (X_1 + X_2 + X_3 + \ldots + X_M)/M = \sum_{i=1}^{M} X_i/M$$

where each X_i is a numerical value and M is the number of values.

Write a BASIC program to find the mean number of sales made by your 20 salespersons last week. The sales were 18, 25, 14, 75, 25, 52, 23, 14, 19, 27, 33, 19, 18, 14, 60, 41, 21, 16, 11 and 51.

```
 5   S=0
10   FOR I= 1 TO 20
15   READ X
20   S=S+X
25   NEXT I
30   M=S/20
35   PRINT "MEAN SALES VALUE IS", M
40   DATA 18, 25, 14, 75, 25, 52, 23, 14, 19, 27
45   DATA 33, 19, 18, 14, 60, 41, 21, 16, 11, 51
50   STOP
55   END
```

The printout is:

MEAN SALES VALUE IS 28.8

The mean is a measure of central tendency. Two other measures of central tendency are the mode (the most frequently occurring value) and the median (the middle value). The mode of the above 20 sales amounts is 14. The median is $(23 + 21)/2 = 22$. The two middle values must be averaged to find the median if there are an even number of values. (If there are an odd number of values, then it is just the middle value.)

Let's assume that our 20 salespersons sold the following amounts: 29, 29, 29, 29, 29, 29, 29, 29, 29, 29, 29, 29, 29, 29, 29, 29, 29, 29, 29 and 29. The mean would be $\bar{X} = 29$ obviously. However, even though $\bar{X} = 28.8$ and $\bar{X} = 29$ indicate that the data is somewhat similar (the averages are about the same), the first group of data has a great deal of deviation from the mean and the second group has none. So what we need is a measure of "how spread out the data is." One measure is the mean absolute deviation, or M.A.D. $= \Sigma |X_i - \bar{X}|/M$. This would seem to be the best measure of deviation. However a more popular one (for reasons to be given shortly) is the "sample standard deviation,"

$$S = \sqrt{\Sigma (X_i - \bar{X})^2/(M - 1)}.$$

Find the M.A.D. and S for the following data: 3, 5, 8, 11, 23.

```
3    T=0
5    DIM X(5)
15   FOR I=1 TO 5
20   READ X(I)
23   T=T+X(I)
25   NEXT I
30   M=T/5
35   FOR J=1 TO 5
40   M1=M1+ABS(X(J)-M)
45   NEXT J
50   M2=M1/5
52   M3=0
55   FOR K=1 TO 5
```

```
60    M3=M3+(X(K)-M)**2
65    NEXT K
70    S=SQR(M3/4)
80    PRINT "MEAN ABSOLUTE DEVIATION IS", M2
90    PRINT "STANDARD DEVIATION IS", S
100   DATA 3, 5, 8, 11, 23
110   STOP
120   END
```

The printout is:

```
MEAN ABSOLUTE DEVIATION IS  5.6
STANDARD DEVIATION IS  7.874008
```

These averages and measures of deviation help to reduce a lot of data into a few manageable pieces of information. But what really is our goal in doing a statistical problem? It's to come up with a conclusion or decision about something unknown, under debate and important. And, it is hoped, to come up with the right decision when a world of possibly incorrect decisions are available.

Decision-Making and Sample Size Problems 3

Let's look at an example and use our BASIC programs and standard normal curve to make the correct decision with a specified level of confidence about a particular problem.

Waycross Limited is having trouble with production at their Fort Street plant. You believe that more vigilant maintenance of the machines and a little better management style could turn things around, but part of the problem is that no one really believes production has dropped off significantly. So you decide to prove it to them.

Over the past three years Fort Street has averaged 100 units per hour. This 100 will be called the true population mean μ (the true standard over time). For the next two weeks you collect the 80 hourly production values and get the following data:

101	87	114	59	70	93	96	102
96	49	120	75	87	88	99	103
93	97	98	94	103	101	85	89
102	90	89	90	97	79	88	94
94	99	95	98	115	42	99	99
97	92	83	83	93	102	100	90
85	97	85	96	94	97	98	99
94	92	91	105	106	91	86	83
89	82	89	95	95	95	57	95
103	109	100	96	95	89	101	87

It turns out that from the central limit theorem the formula $Z = (\overline{X} - \mu)/(S/\sqrt{M})$ is standard normally distributed (if $M > 30$) under repeated sampling. This means for our problem here that the point of contention, whether μ still equals 100, can be tested. If $\mu = 100$, $Z = (\overline{X} - \mu)/(S/\sqrt{M})$ should fall in the middle of the standard normal curve, namely, near zero. Let's write a BASIC program to find out.

```
5         REM TEST THE HYPOTHESIS
10        REM THAT THE TRUE MEAN
15        REM IS STILL ONE HUNDRED
20        DIM X(80)
25        T=0
30        FOR I=1 TO 80
35        READ X(I)
40        T=T+X(I)
50        NEXT I
60        M=T/80.
70        T1=0
75        FOR J=1 TO 80
80        T1=T1+(X(J)-M)**2
90        NEXT J
100       S=SQR(T1/79)
110       Z=(M-100.)/(S/SQR(80.))
115       PRINT M,S
120       PRINT "Z VALUE IS",Z
130       DATA 101, 87, 114, 59, 70, 93, 96, 102
140       DATA 96, 49, 120, 75, 87, 88, 99, 103
150       DATA 93, 97, 98, 94, 103, 101, 85, 89
160       DATA 102, 90, 89, 90, 97, 79, 88, 94
170       DATA 94, 99, 95, 98, 115, 42, 99, 99
180       DATA 97, 92, 83, 83, 93, 102, 100, 90
190       DATA 85, 97, 85, 96, 94, 97, 98, 99
200       DATA 94, 92, 91, 105, 106, 91, 86, 83
210       DATA 89, 82, 89, 95, 95, 95, 57, 95
```

```
220         DATA 103, 109, 100, 96, 95, 89, 101, 87
230         STOP
240         END
RUN
10:56       SEP 12 RUNSBAA . . .
92.3000     12.5349
Z VALUE IS  -5.49433
```

The sample mean (from the eighty readings) is calculated to be $\bar{X}$ = 92.3 with S = 12.5349. When substituted into the Z = $(\bar{X} - \mu)/(S/\sqrt{M})$ formula along with μ = 100 and M − 80, the computer calculated Z to be about −5.49. Now if μ truly is still 100 then $P(-3.0 \leqslant Z \leqslant 3.0)$ = $2P(0 \leqslant Z \leqslant 3.0)$ = 2 × 0.4987 = 0.9974. Therefore if μ is still 100, the Z value should have stood a 99.74% chance of falling between ±3.0. But it didn't. So one of two things has happened: either μ still equals 100 and we observed an incredibly unlikely event, or the hypothesis is wrong, $\mu \neq$ 100, and we have just observed strong evidence that it is wrong. We will go with the latter explanation and be almost absolutely certain that μ has dropped (no longer 100).

Now one could say, I see that the sample mean is 92.3 so I think the mean has dropped. What's wrong with that? Nothing. But by doing the extra statistical analysis we get the odds of being right or wrong. And in this case the odds are way above 99% for rejecting the old standard of μ = 100.

Therefore, Waycross Limited really does have a production problem at their Fort Street plant and corrective steps should be taken.

What we just did is called a *classical statistical test of hypothesis*, and we will do more of these later. However, sometimes statisticians like to present their results in something called a *confidence interval*. So let's derive one for the previous problem.

As just stated, we have $P(-3.0 \leqslant Z \leqslant 3.0) = 0.9974$ for a standard normal variable Z. Therefore $P(-3.0 \leqslant (\bar{X} - \mu)/(S/\sqrt{M}) \leqslant 3.0) = 0.9974$ as long as $M > 30$. Now we go to work on the inequalities inside $P(\ )$. $P(-3S/\sqrt{M} \leqslant \bar{X} - \mu \leqslant 3S/\sqrt{M}) = 0.9974$ and $P(-\bar{X} - 3S/\sqrt{M} \leqslant -\mu \leqslant -\bar{X} + 3S/\sqrt{M}) = 0.9974$. Now multiplying through by -1 we have $P(\bar{X} + 3S/\sqrt{M} \geqslant \mu \geqslant \bar{X} - 3S/\sqrt{M}) = 0.9974$. What this says is that as long as $M > 30$ the true mean μ stands a 99.74% chance of being between $\bar{X} \pm 3S/\sqrt{M}$. In this case

```
 3   M=92.3000
 5   N=80
10   S=12.5349
15   B=3*S/SQR(80.)
18   PRINT M-B, M+B
20   PRINT B
25   STOP
30   END
```

The printout is:

```
88.09567                    96.50433
4.204333
```

Therefore, Waycross can be 99.74% sure that the true mean at Fort Street is between 88.1 and 96.5. Note that this leads us to the same conclusion as before—that there is a problem at Fort Street. Which is better—a confidence interval or a test of hypothesis? It is strictly a matter of style. Both are commonly used, and both convey the necessary information.

We want to look at some more applied statistical problems, but first let's consider how we solved the Fort Street problem. The 80 sample readings were just presented to us and we went to work on them. This frequently happens in business and science applications. Someone walks into your office with the data and you decide how to analyze it and perform the appropriate statistical test.

____HOW LARGE A SAMPLE?

It could happen that you are put in charge of the study in the beginning. Your boss might say, go over to Fort Street and get some data and do a statistical test to find out for sure if there is a problem or not. So the question is how large a sample should you take. The sample mean $\bar{X}$ converges to the true mean μ as M goes to infinity. From a purely theoretical viewpoint an infinite sample would be nice, but that's impossible. It took 2 weeks just to get the 80 hourly readings.

What your boss really wants is the maximum amount of information with minimum time and cost. How large a sample should be taken can be calculated fairly precisely by studying the derivation of that confidence interval. We only have to specify a few things. Let's pose the question this way: How large a sample should we take at Fort Street in order to be 99% sure that our sample mean $\bar{X}$ will be within four units of the true but unknown mean μ? Therefore $P(-2.575 \leqslant Z \leqslant 2.575) = 0.99$. (Note that from our standard normal chart $0.99/2 = 0.495$ is the appropriate area from 0 to the upper bound. 2.57 gives an area of 0.4949, and 2.58 gives an area of 0.4951. So 2.575 is pretty close. And -2.575 should be the lower bound due to the complete symmetry of the standard normal curve about 0.)

So $P(-2.575 \leqslant Z \leqslant 2.575) = 0.99$ and $P(-2.575 \leqslant (X - \mu)/(S/\sqrt{M}) \leqslant 2.575) = 0.99$; therefore $P(-2.575\, S/\sqrt{M} \leqslant (\bar{X} - \mu) \leqslant 2.575\, S/\sqrt{M}) = 0.99$ so $P(-\bar{X} - 2.575\, S/\sqrt{M} \leqslant -\mu \leqslant -\bar{X} + 2.575\, S/\sqrt{M}) = 0.99$, thus $P(\bar{X} + 2.575\, S/\sqrt{M} \geqslant \mu \geqslant \bar{X}$

− 2.575 $S/\sqrt{M}$) = 0.99. Similar to our previous confidence interval problem, we have a 99% chance that the true mean μ is between $\overline{X}$ − 2.575 $S/\sqrt{M}$ and $\overline{X}$ + 2.575 $S/\sqrt{M}$. Now we require an estimate of S in order to solve for the sample size M. This is usually easily obtained with a preliminary sample of 30 or so; or the quality control engineer will probably know from past records. Failing that, just put an upper bound on S and use that. For this problem let's say that S won't exceed 15. We'll use 15 for S.

Now notice that the ± term (2.575 × 15/$\sqrt{M}$) goes to zero as M goes to infinity. But we want it to go to 4, because that is how close we want it to get to. So we have

$$4 = 2.575 \times 15/\sqrt{M} \quad \text{or}$$

$$\sqrt{M} = 2.575 \times 15/4 \quad \text{or}$$

$$\sqrt{M} = 9.65625 \quad \text{so}$$

$$M = (9.65625)^2 \quad \text{or}$$

$$M = 93.24316$$

Rounded up, we get 94 readings that will produce an $\overline{X}$ that stands a 99% chance of being within four units of the true but unknown mean as long as S is less than or equal to 15. If $\overline{X}$ (from the 94 readings) is less than 96, Fort Street production is in trouble. Solving for the appropriate sample size before doing the study can save time and money and guarantee an acceptable level of results ahead of time.

Notice that we really produced a general formula here for the sample size for the mean of one population when $M > 30$ and S can be estimated (or an upper bound placed on it). It is

$$M = (ZS/B)^2$$

where Z is the appropriate standard normal value for the appropriate confidence level, S is the standard deviation and B is the bound (how close you want to get to the true mean).

Remember, if $M = (ZS/B)^2$ is less than 30, the value 30 should be used because $Z = (\overline{X} - \mu)/(S/\sqrt{M})$ is only standard normally distributed if $M > 30$.

Instead of having to figure this out each time, let's write a BASIC program to produce a "sample size chart." Let's produce sample sizes for 85%, 90%, 95%, 98% and 99% confidence levels. We'll let the bounds (B) vary from 0.1 to 0.5 to 1 to 2 to 3 to 4 to 5 to 10 to 15 to 20. Also, S will vary from 1 to 3 to 5 to 7 to 9 to 11 to 13 to 15.

Look up the 85, 90, 95, 98 and 99% confidence bounds on our previously produced standard normal chart:

Value of Z

0.85/2 = 0.425	1.44
0.90/2 = 0.45	1.645
0.95/2 = 0.475	1.96
0.98/2 = 0.49	2.33
0.99/2 = 0.495	2.575

Also note in the program that PRINT by itself leaves a blank space, and PRINTUSING controls the spacing and decimals of the printed information. Arrange these (### represents places) to suit your requirements.

The program and printout follow:

```
5    REM SAMPLE SIZE CHART
10   DIM N(5), Z(5), B(10)
20   FOR J=1 TO 5
```

```
25    READ Z(J)
30    NEXT J
35    FOR K=1 TO 10
40    READ B(K)
43    NEXT K
44    FOR S=1 TO 15 STEP 2
45    PRINT "STANDARD DEVIATION=", S
46    PRINT "           ", "HOW SURE"
47    PRINTUSING 48, "BOUND", 85, 90, 95, 98, 99
48:   ###### #####. ######. ######. ######. ######.
55    FOR L=1 TO 10
60    FOR M=1 TO 5
70    N(M)=INT(((Z(M)*S)/B(L))**2+1.)
80    IF N(M) < 30 THEN 100
90    GO TO 110
100   N(M)=30
110   NEXT M
120   PRINTUSING 130, B(L), N(1), N(2), N(3), N(4), N(5)
130:  ###.# ######. ######. ######. ######. ######.
135   PRINT
140   NEXT L
145   PRINT
146   PRINT
147   PRINT
148   PRINT
149   PRINT
150   NEXT S
160   DATA 1.44, 1.645, 1.96, 2.33, 2.575
170   DATA .1, .5, 1, 2, 3, 4, 5, 10, 15, 20
180   STOP
190   END
RUN
```

STANDARD DEVIATION= 1

		HOW SURE			
BOUND	85.	90.	95.	98.	99.
0.1	208.	271.	385.	543.	664.
0.5	30.	30.	30.	30.	30.
1.0	30.	30.	30.	30.	30.
2.0	30.	30.	30.	30.	30.
3.0	30.	30.	30.	30.	30.
4.0	30.	30.	30.	30.	30.
5.0	30.	30.	30.	30.	30.
10.0	30.	30.	30.	30.	30.
15.0	30.	30.	30.	30.	30.
20.0	30.	30.	30.	30.	30.

STANDARD DEVIATION= 3

		HOW SURE			
BOUND	85.	90.	95.	98.	99.
0.1	1867.	2436.	3458.	4887.	5968.
0.5	75.	98.	139.	196.	239.
1.0	30.	30.	35.	49.	60.
2.0	30.	30.	30.	30.	30.
3.0	30.	30.	30.	30.	30.
4.0	30.	30.	30.	30.	30.
5.0	30.	30.	30.	30.	30.
10.0	30.	30.	30.	30.	30.
15.0	30.	30.	30.	30.	30.
20.0	30.	30.	30.	30.	30.

STANDARD DEVIATION=   5

HOW SURE

BOUND	85.	90.	95.	98.	99.
0.1	5184.	6766.	9604.	13573.	16577.
0.5	208.	271.	385.	543.	664.
1.0	52.	68.	97.	136.	166.
2.0	30.	30.	30.	34.	42.
3.0	30.	30.	30.	30.	30.
4.0	30.	30.	30.	30.	30.
5.0	30.	30.	30.	30.	30.
10.0	30.	30.	30.	30.	30.
15.0	30.	30.	30.	30.	30.
20.0	30.	30.	30.	30.	30.

STANDARD DEVIATION=   7

HOW SURE

BOUND	85.	90.	95.	98.	99.
0.1	10161.	13260.	18824.	26602.	32491.
0.5	407.	531.	753.	1065.	1300.
1.0	102.	133.	189.	267.	325.
2.0	30.	34.	48.	67.	82.
3.0	30.	30.	30.	30.	37.
4.0	30.	30.	30.	30.	30.
5.0	30.	30.	30.	30.	30.
10.0	30.	30.	30.	30.	30.
15.0	30.	30.	30.	30.	30.
20.0	30.	30.	30.	30.	30.

STANDARD DEVIATION=   9
                        HOW SURE

BOUND	85.	90.	95.	98.	99.
0.1	16797.	21919.	31117.	43975.	53709.
0.5	672.	877.	1245.	1759.	2149.
1.0	168.	220.	312.	440.	538.
2.0	42.	55.	78.	110.	135.
3.0	30.	30.	35.	49.	60.
4.0	30.	30.	30.	30.	34.
5.0	30.	30.	30.	30.	30.
10.0	30.	30.	30.	30.	30.
15.0	30.	30.	30.	30.	30.
20.0	30.	30.	30.	30.	30.

STANDARD DEVIATION=   11
                        HOW SURE

BOUND	85.	90.	95.	98.	99.
0.1	25091.	32743.	46484.	65690.	80231.
0.5	1004.	1310.	1860.	2628.	3210.
1.0	251.	328.	465.	657.	803.
2.0	63.	82.	117	165	201.
3.0	30.	37.	52.	73.	90.
4.0	30.	30.	30.	42.	51.
5.0	30.	30.	30.	30.	33.
10.0	30.	30.	30.	30.	30.
15.0	30.	30.	30.	30.	30.
20.0	30.	30.	30.	30.	30.

STANDARD DEVIATION=   13

		HOW SURE			
BOUND	85.	90.	95.	98.	99.
0.1	35044.	45732.	64924.	91749.	112058.
0.5	1402.	1830.	2597.	3670.	4483.
1.0	351.	458.	650.	918.	1121.
2.0	88.	115.	163.	230.	281.
3.0	39.	51.	73.	102.	125.
4.0	30.	30.	41.	58.	71.
5.0	30.	30.	30.	37.	45.
10.0	30.	30.	30.	30.	30.
15.0	30.	30.	30.	30.	30.
20.0	30.	30.	30.	30.	30.

STANDARD DEVIATION=   15

		HOW SURE			
BOUND	85.	90.	95.	98.	99.
0.1	46656.	60886.	86436.	122151.	149190.
0.5	1867.	2436.	3458.	4887.	5968.
1.0	467.	609.	865.	1222.	1492.
2.0	117.	153.	217.	306.	373.
3.0	52.	68.	97.	136.	166.
4.0	30.	39.	55.	77.	94.
5.0	30.	30.	35.	49.	60.
10.0	30.	30.	30.	30.	30.
15.0	30.	30.	30.	30.	30.
20.0	30.	30.	30.	30.	30.

Of course, different bounds, confidence level values and *S* values can be read in to suit the sampler's needs.

_____EXERCISES

3.1. How many grade A wooden beams should Grand Marais West's quality control engineer measure in order to be 95% sure that the sample mean $\overline{X}$ is within 0.1 of the true but unknown mean length? S is estimated to be 1.

3.2. How many industrial grade AA light bulbs should the Michigan Valley Light Bulb Company test (to see how many days they last) in order to be 99% sure that their sample mean $(\overline{X})$ length of life is within three days of the true but unknown mean? (Preliminary tests have put the S value at 15.) Keeping the sample size small here is vital because the test destroys the sample.

3.3. The quality control computer at Lordsburg Dening Controls Group will be assisting in measuring grade AAA bolts for width as they are manufactured. How many bolts must be measured in each batch in order to be 98% sure that the sample mean is within 0.1 of the true but unknown mean width of the bolts? S has been three units in the past.

More 4
Statistical Applications

____A TWO-POPULATION TEST

The Okemos Manufacturing Group has been testing two different production processes for product XK5. Their goal is to choose the better of the two processes for all of their XK5 manufacturing plants. The only measure of effectiveness they care about is quality (less defectives).

The data has just come in. The first plant, using production process 1, had daily number of defective XK5's for 50 days as follows: 41, 52, 19, 18, 37, 62, 14, 75, 31, 29, 63, 17, 18, 14, 11, 52, 25, 16, 18, 75, 4, 19, 28, 26, 15, 11, 10, 6, 42, 35, 8, 14, 3, 18, 26, 32, 27, 31, 14, 12, 35, 16, 19, 29, 32, 33, 17, 50, 10 and 21.

The second plant, using production process 2, had daily number of defective XK5's for 50 days as follows: 31, 37, 39, 41, 48, 51, 19, 29, 34, 42, 30, 42, 25, 39, 35, 47, 49, 25, 27, 28, 41, 47, 50, 26, 21, 20, 38, 31, 41, 52, 14, 19, 34, 26, 34, 23, 62, 51, 49, 60, 18, 27, 35, 41, 40, 52, 37, 50, 43 and 55.

The means and standard deviations can be easily calculated, and the smaller mean could be judged to represent the better

47

quality process. But management wants to be certain; much
is at stake in time, money and the company's reputation.
It turns out that

$$Z = ((\overline{X}_1 - \overline{X}_2) - (\mu_1 - \mu_2))/\sqrt{S_1^2/M_1 + S_2^2/M_2}$$

is standard normally distributed if $M_1 + M_2 > 30$. They decide
to test the hypothesis that $\mu_1 = \mu_2$ against the alternative that
$\mu_1 \neq \mu_2$ at the $\alpha = 0.01$ level. That means they will reject the
hypothesis that $\mu_1 = \mu_2$ only if they are 99% sure that it is
untrue. So $0.99/2 = 0.495$. From our standard normal table
2.575 is the Z value such that the area from 0 to 2.575 is
0.495. Therefore, we write a BASIC program to do the

$$Z = ((\overline{X}_1 - \overline{X}_2) - (\mu_1 - \mu_2))/\sqrt{S_1^2/M_1 + S_2^2/M_2}$$

calculation assuming that $\mu_1 = \mu_2$ (therefore $\mu_1 - \mu_2 = 0$). If
$\mu_1 = \mu_2$ (quality the same), we stand a 99% chance that the
formula value will be between ±2.575. The program follows:

```
5    REM TEST TO SEE IF
10   REM THERE IS A REAL
20   REM DIFFERENCE IN
30   REM QUALITY PERFORMANCE
40   REM BETWEEN THE TWO
50   REM PRODUCTION PROCESSES
60   DIM X(50), Y(50)
70   T1=0
80   T2=0
90   FOR I=1 TO 50
100  READ X(I)
110  T1=T1+X(I)
120  NEXT I
130  FOR J=1 TO 50
140  READ Y(J)
```

```
150   T2=T2+Y(J)
160   NEXT J
170   M1=T1/50.
180   M2=T2/50.
190   R1=0
200   R2=0
210   FOR K=1 TO 50
220   R1=R1+(X(K)-M1)**2
230   R2=R2+(Y(K)-M2)**2
240   NEXT K
250   S1=SQR(R1/49.)
260   S2=SQR(R2/49.)
270   Z=(M1-M2-0)/SQR(S1**2/50.+S2**2/50.)
280   PRINT "FIRST GRP MEAN STD ARE", M1, S1
290   PRINT "SECOND GRP MEAN STD ARE", M2, S2
300   PRINT "Z VALUE IS", Z
310   REM FIRST GROUP DEFECTIVES
320   DATA 41, 52, 19, 18, 37, 62, 14, 75, 31, 29
330   DATA 63, 17, 18, 14, 11, 52, 25, 16, 18, 75
340   DATA 4, 19, 28, 26, 15, 11, 10, 6, 42, 35
350   DATA 8, 14, 3, 18, 26, 32, 27, 31, 14, 12
360   DATA 35, 16, 19, 29, 32, 33, 17, 50, 10, 21
370   REM SECOND GROUP DEFECTIVES
380   DATA 31, 37, 39, 41, 48, 51, 19, 29, 34, 42
390   DATA 30, 42, 25, 39, 35, 47, 49, 25, 27, 28
400   DATA 41, 47, 50, 26, 21, 20, 38, 31, 41, 52
410   DATA 14, 19, 34, 26, 34, 23, 62, 51, 49, 60
420   DATA 18, 27, 35, 41, 40, 52, 37, 50, 43, 55
430   STOP
440   END
RUN
```

```
FIRST GRP MEAN STD ARE      26.6000    17.3311
SECOND GRP MEAN STD ARE     37.1000    11.7321
Z VALUE IS    -3.54758
```

Therefore $Z = -3.54758$ which is way outside the 99% area bounded by ± 2.575. We have observed an event that could almost never happen if $\mu_1 = \mu_2$. The quality is quite different and the first plant's production process yields many fewer defective XK5's. So production process 1 should be adopted, with little fear that Okemos made the wrong decision.

In general, in any statistical test two hypotheses are asserted and then an experiment (with the correct formula) is conducted to see which one is more believable, based on the sample.

_____EXERCISES

4.1. Derive a 99% confidence interval for $\mu_1 - \mu_2$ for the Okemos Manufacturing Group problem.

4.2. Could sample sizes (M_1 and M_2) be calculated (similar to the one-sample problem) to meet certain requirements?

_____PROPORTION PROBLEMS

$Z = (P - \pi)/\sqrt{\pi(1 - \pi)/M}$ is also standard normally distributed if $M > 30$, where P is the sample proportion and π is the true proportion.

The Madisonville-Portland Plant has been running a 3% defective rate on its KXC product that it manufactures. Recently management expressed concerns that the defective rate was increasing. A sample of $M = 10,000$ KXC products revealed 341 defectives. We will test at the $\propto - 0.05$ level for an increase in the defective rate. The old standard is usually called the null hypothesis and written as H_0; the alternative hypothesis is denoted by H_A. So we are testing

$H_0 : \pi = 0.03$ versus $H_A : \pi > 0.03$

This is called a one-sided test and all of the 0.05 rejection region probability is put in the upper end of the normal curve (due to the "greater than" alternative). When we look up 0.45 area under our normal curve, we see that 1.645 is the upper 0.05 point. If the calculated formula value is greater than 1.645, we will reject H_0 and conclude that the company has problems (defective rate has increased).

```
 5   REM TEST TO SEE IF .03
10   REM DEFECTIVE RATE IS
15   REM STILL ACCURATE
20   P=341/10000.
25   P1=.03
30   Z=(P-P1)/SQR((P1*(1-P1))/10000)
35   PRINT Z
40   STOP
45   END
```

The printout is:

2.40346

So we reject $H_0 : \pi = 0.03$ because $2.40346 > 1.645$ and we are at least 95% sure that the defective rate has increased.

The West Iron County Retailers Group requires a 98% confidence interval for their proportion of market share for product ZA12. Derive this if a sample of 100 customers yielded 24 who had purchased ZA12 from them and 76 who had purchased a similar product from their competitors.

We have $P(-2.33 \leqslant Z \leqslant 2.33) = 0.98$, therefore $P(-2.33 \leqslant (P - \pi)/\sqrt{\pi(1-\pi)/M} \leqslant 2.33) = 0.98$. Thus $P(-2.33\sqrt{\pi(1-\pi/M} \leqslant P - \pi \leqslant 2.33\sqrt{\pi(1-\pi)/M}) = 0.98$. So $P(-P - 2.33\sqrt{\pi(1-\pi)/M} \leqslant -\pi \leqslant -P + 2.33\sqrt{\pi(1-\pi)/M}) = 0.98$, therefore $P(P + 2.33\sqrt{\pi(1-\pi/M} \geqslant \pi \geqslant P - 2.33\sqrt{\pi(1-\pi)/M}) = 0.98$.

Therefore, the true proportion π stands a 98% chance of being between $\pm 2.33\sqrt{\pi(1-\pi)/M}$. But we have to get rid of $\pi(1-\pi)$ because we can't have π bounded by a function of π. We get around this by finding π between 0 and 1 such that $\pi(1-\pi)$ is a maximum (this will give us a safe bound). Write a BASIC program to find the maximum of $f(X) = X(1-X)$ subject to $0 \leqslant X \leqslant 1$. The program follows:

```
5     REM MAXIMIZE A FUNCTION
10    REM OF ONE VARIABLE
15    B=-9999999
20    FOR X=0 TO 1 STEP .001
30    F=X*(1-X)
40    IF F > B THEN 60
50    GO TO 80
60    A1=X
70    B=F
80    NEXT X
90    PRINT "F IS MAXIMIZED AT", A1
100   STOP
110   END
```

The printout is:

```
F IS MAXIMIZED AT    .5000000
```

Our bound is $2.33\sqrt{0.5(1-0.5)/M}$, or in our case $2.33\sqrt{0.25/100} = 0.1165$. So the company is 98% sure that its true proportion is within 0.24 ± 0.1165. That seems like a pretty wide confidence interval, but more samples and/or less confidence would narrow it as required.

Now let's look at that bound again: $(2.33\sqrt{0.5^2/M})$. For any appropriate confidence level it could be written as $Z\sqrt{0.5^2/M}$. Let's set this equal to a bound B and solve for M as in our previous sample size problems with means. We have

$B = Z\sqrt{0.5^2/M}$ or

$B^2 = Z^2 (0.5^2/M)$ then

$M = Z^2 (0.5^2/B^2)$ or

$M = (Z\, 0.5/B)^2$ therefore

$M = (Z/2B)^2$

As an example, how large a sample would West Iron County Retailers Group have to take in order to be 98% sure that their sample proportion P was within 0.01 of the true but unknown proportion π? From the formula we get $M = (Z/2B)^2$ so

```
 5   Z=2.33
10   B-.01
15   N=INT((Z/(2*B))**2+1)
20   REM ROUNDING N UP
25   PRINT "SAMPLE SIZE IS", N
30   STOP
35   END
```

The printout is:

       SAMPLE SIZE IS   13573

They must sample 13,573 customers to be that sure and that close.

Let's write a BASIC program to construct a sample size chart for proportions for 85, 90, 95, 98 and 99% confidence with proportion bounds of 0.005, 0.010, 0.015, 0.020, 0.025, . . . , up to 0.200. The program follows:

```
5    REM SAMPLE SIZE CHART
7    REM FOR PROPORTIONS
10   DIM N(5), Z(5)
20   FOR J=1 TO 5
25   READ Z(J)
30   NEXT J
46   PRINT "      ", "HOW SURE"
47   PRINTUSING 48, "BOUND", 85, 90, 95, 98, 99
48:  ###### #####. #####. ######. ######. ######.
55   FOR B=.005 TO .20 STEP .005
60   FOR M=1 TO 5
70   N(M)=INT((Z(M)/(2*B))**2+1.)
80   IF N(M) < 30 THEN 100
90   GO TO 110
100  N(M)=30
110  NEXT M
120  PRINTUSING 130, B, N(1), N(2), N(3), N(4), N(5)
130: .#### ######. ######. ######. ######. ######.
135  PRINT
140  NEXT B
160  DATA 1.44, 1.645, 1.96, 2.33, 2.575
170  STOP
180  END
```

The printout is:

			HOW SURE		
BOUND	85.	90.	95.	98.	99.
.0050	20736.	27061.	38416.	54290.	66307.
.0100	5184.	6766.	9604.	13573.	16577.

.0150	2304.	3007.	4269.	6033.	7368.
.0200	1296.	1692.	2401.	3394.	4145.
.0250	830.	1083.	1537.	2172.	2653.
.0300	576.	752.	1068.	1509.	1842.
.0350	424.	553.	785.	1108.	1354.
.0400	324.	423.	601.	849.	1037.
.0450	257.	335.	475.	671.	819.
.0500	208.	271.	385.	543.	664.
.0550	172.	224.	318.	449.	548.
.0600	145.	188.	267.	378.	461.
.0650	123.	161.	228.	322.	393.
.0700	106.	139.	197.	277.	339.
.0750	93.	121.	171.	242.	295.
.0800	82.	106.	151.	213.	260.
.0850	72.	94.	133.	188.	230.
.0900	65.	84.	119.	168.	205.
.0950	58.	75.	107.	151.	184.
.1000	52.	68.	97.	136.	166.
.1050	48.	62.	88.	124.	151.
.1100	43.	56.	80.	113.	137.
.1150	40.	52.	73.	103.	126.
.1200	37.	47.	67.	95.	116.
.1250	34.	44.	62.	87.	107.
.1300	31.	41.	57.	81.	99.
.1350	30.	38.	53.	75.	91.
.1400	30.	35.	50.	70.	85.
.1450	30.	33.	46.	65.	79.
.1500	30.	31.	43.	61.	74.
.1550	30.	30.	40.	57.	69.

.1600	30.	30.	38.	54.	65.
.1650	30.	30.	36.	50.	61.
.1700	30.	30.	34.	47.	58.
.1750	30.	30.	32.	45.	55.
.1800	30.	30.	30.	42.	52.
.1850	30.	30.	30.	40.	49.
.1900	30.	30.	30.	38.	46.
.1950	30.	30.	30.	36.	44.
.2000	30.	30.	30.	34.	42.

_____**EXERCISES**

4.3. The West Branch Mountain Plant has just purchased 1,000,000 Grade C bolts. Their supplier has made guarantees about the defective rate. But West Branch wants to check the defective rate on their own. How many bolts must they check in order to be 95% sure that their sample proportion of defectives (P) is within 0.01 of the true proportion of defectives π?

4.4. Fort Dawson Market Researchers needs to estimate market share for a client. They are guaranteeing 90% confidence to within 0.02 of the true proportion π. How many customers must they interview?

4.5. Crystal Falls Manistique Plant has been sponsoring a top-rated television show for years. They are paying ten million dollars a year for the privilege and they have been guaranteed by the show that they are getting a 30% market share. However, Mr. O'Hara (Crystal Falls' President) believes that the inroads made by cable and super satellite stations have cut into his 30% market share. The contract is up for renewal. Mr. O'Hara has been assured by Fast Freddie (the show's promoter) that the 30% market share is still holding. Because Fast Freddie has had a rather checkered career, Mr. O'Hara decides to have his own people do a telephone survey during the show before he commits ten million dollars for another year. He wants to be within 3% with his sample proportion and 99% sure. According to our chart how many telephone interviews should discover whether Fast Freddie was being fast or not?

Market Research 5

The preceding chapter dealt with population sample size problems. However, frequently in business or science, multiple population sample sizes must be determined. If one desires an overall confidence level for the entire group of populations, then the problem becomes more interesting and sophisticated. We present the Michigan South Coast Corporation case as an example.

Note: DIM X(100) in **BASIC** declares $X(1), X(3), \ldots, X(100)$ as variables ready for use in a program. RND(X) produces random numbers between 0 and 1. And

$$\prod_{i=1}^{5} X_i = X_1 X_2 X_3 X_4 X_5$$

is the product notation.

The Michigan South Coast Corporation is gearing up for production and sales of its five products for the coming year. Products 1 through 5 are sold in five different parts of the country, but they are manufactured at South Coast's Santa Fe plant. Therefore the company has the problem of trying to decide how much of each of the five products to make for the coming year. Due to current interest rates, some skilled labor shortages and storage costs, South Coast wants to be fairly accurate in its forecasts. It has decided to proceed as follows: It will take telephone interviews of potential customers in its five product sales territories. The individual interviews for products 1 through 5 will take 18, 9, 5, 7 and 12 minutes, respectively allowing a little time for busy signals and other minor delays. Management wants the sample proportion who say they will buy product i ($i = 1, 2, \ldots, 5$) (adjusted for certain factors and responses) to be within 0.01, 0.02, 0.025, 0.015 and 0.03, respectively, of the true but unknown proportion of buyers. Also, management wants to be at least 90% sure of these individual results. However $0.90^5 = 0.59$, so there is concern that even though they would be 90% sure on each confidence interval, there is a 40% chance that at least one of the intervals would be wrong. This is unacceptable to management because of the amount of money at stake. So they place the additional condition that the probability of all the confidence intervals holding must be at least 0.80. Preliminary sampling and past results indicate that $n_i = (Z_i/2B_i)^2$ would be an appropriate individual sample size formula for this problem, where Z_i is the appropriate normal value and B_i is the appropriate bound. (This formula can be varied or another can be substituted as circumstances dictate.) So we have minimize

$$c = \sum_{i=1}^{5} T_i(Z_i/2B_i)^2$$

subject to all standard normal values Z_i which must have corresponding P_i greater than 0.4500 (the 90% bound) and

$$\prod_{i=1}^{5} (2P_i) \geqslant 0.80,$$

each $(Z_i/2B_i)^2 > 30$ and $T_1 = 18$, $T_2 = 9$, $T_3 = 5$, $T_4 = 7$, $T_5 = 12$, $B_1 = 0.01$, $B_2 = 0.02$, $B_3 = 0.025$, $B_4 = 0.015$ and $B_5 = 0.03$. The multistage program, solution and explanation follow:

```
1    DIM H(5), N(5), L(5), A(5), B(5), U(5)
2    DIM X(5, 136), P(5, 136)
3    M=9999999
4    B1=.01, B2=.02, B3=.025, B4=0.15, B5=.03
5    F=2, G=.8
6    FOR I1=1 TO 5
7    B(I1)=1
8    A(I1)=68
9    N(I1)=136
10   NEXT I1
12   X=1
14   FOR I3=1 TO 136
15   READ E
16   FOR I2=1 TO 5
17   X(I2, I3)=1.64+.01*I3
18   P(I2, I3)=2*E
19   NEXT I2
20   NEXT I3
21   FOR J=1 TO 8
22   FOR I=1 TO 1500
24   FOR K=1 TO 5
30   IF A(K)-N(K)/F**)J-1) < B(K) THEN 50
40   GO TO 60
50   L(K)=B(K)
55   GO TO 65
60   L(K)=A(K)-N(K)/F**(J-1)
65   IF A(K)+N(K)/F**(J-1) > N(K) THEN 80
70   GO TO 90
80   U(K)=N(K)-L(K)
85   GO TO 100
90   U(K)=A(K)+N(K)/F**(J-1)-L(K)
```

```
100   H(K)=INT(L(K)+RND(X)*U(K))
102   NEXT K
104   Z1=H(1), Z2=H(2), Z3=H(3), Z4=h(4), Z5=H(5)
106   P9=P(1, Z1)*P(2, Z2)*P(3, Z3)*P(4, Z4)*P(5, Z5)
108   IF P9 < G THEN 170
110   C1=18*(X(1, Z1)/(2*B1))**2
112   C2=9*(X(2, Z2)/(2*B2))**2
114   C3=5*(X(3, Z3)/(2*B3))**2
116   C4=7*(X(4, Z4)/(2*B4))**2
118   C5=12*(X(5, Z5)/(2*B5))**2
120   C=C1+C2+C3+C4+C5
122   IF C < M THEN 160
150   GO TO 170
160   A(1)=H(1), A(2)=H(2), A(3)=H(3), A(4)=H(4), A(5)=H(5), M=C
162   D1=C1, D2=C2, D3=C3, D4=C4, D5=C5
164   P0=P9
170   NEXT I
175   PRINT A(1), A(2), A(3), A(4), A(5), M
180   NEXT J
190   PRINT D1, D2, D3, D4, D5
200   PRINT M, "OVERALL PROBABILITY IS", P0
204   REM A MULTI STAGE MONTE CARLO
208   REM OPTIMIZATION EXAMPLE
210   DATA .4505, .4515, .4525, .4535, .4545
220   DATA .4554, .4564, .4573, .4582, .4591, .4599, .4608, .4616, .4625, .4633
230   DATA .4641, .4649, .4656, .4664, .4671, .4678, .4686, .4693, .4699, .4706
235   DATA .4713, .4719, .4726, .4732, .4738, .4744, .4750, .4756, .4761, .4767
240   DATA .4772, .4778, .4783, .4788, .4793, .4798, .4803, .4808, .4812, .4817
245   DATA .4821, .4826, .4830, .4834, .4838, .4842, .4846, .4850, .4854, .4857
250   DATA .4861, .4864, .4868, .4871, .4875, .4878, .4881, .4884, .4887, .4890
255   DATA .4893, .4896, .4898, .4901, .4904, .4906, .4909, .4911, .4913, .4916
260   DATA .4918, .4920, .4022, .4925, .4927, .4929, .4931, .4932, .4934, .4936
265   DATA .4938, .4940, .4941, .4943, .4945, .4946, .4948, .4949, .4951, .4952
270   DATA .4953, .4955, .4956, .4957, .4959, .4960, .4961, .4962, .4963, .4964
275   DATA .4965, .4966, .4967, .4968, .4969, .4970, .4971, .4972, .4973, .4974
280   DATA .4974, .4975, .4976, .4977, .4977, .4978, .4979, .4979, .4980, .4981
290   DATA .4981, .4982, .4983, .4983, .4984, .4984, .4985, .4985, .4986, .4986
295   DATA .4987,
310   STOP
320   END
```

The printout is:

Subscripts	1	83	84	25	74
function value	215795.				
"	1	49	99	57	53

"	215550.				
"	2	44	97	29	80
"	210779.				
"	1	49	98	43	48
"	210070.				
"	1	47	104	32	61
"	208674.				
"	1	45	89	34	67
"	208164.				
"	1	45	87	35	66
"	208117.				
"	1	45	87	35	66
"	208117.				
"	122512.	24570.6	12600.2	30800.8	17633.3
Solution	208117.	OVERALL PROBABILITY IS			.800145

After changing line 22 to FOR I=1 TO 10000, we obtain the true optimal solution given in the following printout:

Subscripts	2	59	75	52	41
function value	213695.				
"	2	54	56	38	72
"	210716.				
"	1	41	83	36	80
"	209310.				
"	1	42	80	37	72
"	208278.				
"	1	49	82	33	67
"	208108.				
"	1	48	81	34	67
"	208077.				
"	1	47	80	35	67
"	208051.				
"	1	47	80	35	67
"	208051.				
"	122512.	25043.1	11907.2	30800.8	17787.0
Solution	208051.	OVERALL PROBABILITY IS			.800021

Therefore the optimal solution is:

122,512 minutes spent interviewing (122,512/18) people in market 1
25,043.1 minutes spent interviewing (25,043.1/9) people in market 2
11,907.2 minutes spent interviewing (11,907.2/5) people in market 3
30,800.8 minutes spent interviewing (30,800.8/7) people in market 4
17,787 minutes spent interviewing (17,787/12) people in market 5

A grand total of 208,051 minutes will be spent interviewing, and the probability of meeting all the confidence interval bounds is 0.800021 as required.

Without using multistage, we would be forced into solving for sample sizes in a somewhat less than optimal way. For example, $0.80^{0.2} = 0.9564$. We could meet the 0.80 overall confidence and the individual at least 90% confidences (on the bounds) by using the corresponding normal value $Z = 2.02$ (for the 0.9564). This leads to total samples of 20, 054 versus 17,856 with the multistage Monte Carlo constrained optimal solution. This represents an 11% reduction in samples with our optimal solution. Also, with the interview time weights put in, the overall time savings is 20%.

Remember that the multistage process is flexible. It could handle many other multiple population sampling scheme problems. This could be an interesting area for further research.

A brief explanation of the previous multistage BASIC computer program follows. The function is in lines 110 through 120. As the bounds on the confidence interval sizes are fixed in line 4 and the time weights are in the function, this function depends on (and hence is a function of) the appropriate standard normal Z_i values which we call $X(I, J)$ in the program (where I refers to the population and the J refers to ranked normal probabilities from $J = 1$ (0.4505) to $J = 2$ (0.4515), ... ,

$J = 136\,(0.4987)$. These probability values are read in lines 14 through 20. The actual data from a standard normal table is in lines 210 through 295. The probabilities are doubled and assigned to $P(I, J)$ in line 18, while their corresponding Z values (for the function evaluation) are fixed in line 17.

Lines 21 through 102 create and control the five-dimensional rectangles that are reduced in size seven times. Each new-size rectangle is sampled 1,500 times (10,000 times in our true optimal run), each time storing the best answer so far and constantly repositioning the rectangles about the best answer so far. In addition, our

$$\mathop{\pi}_{i=1}^{5} (2P_i) \geqslant 0.80$$

must be checked in line 108 to see that it holds.

Note: In this problem if

$$\mathop{\pi}_{i=1}^{5} (2P_i) < 0.80,$$

the answer was thrown out. Doing this led to only 50,000 of the 80,000 sample answers in the $8 \times 10,000$ run being feasible. This was more than enough to solve the problem. However, in more sophisticated circumstances we might want to shrink or expand all sample solutions so that they are all feasible, if efficiency dictates. (This is sometimes easy and sometimes very difficult to do.)

Notice that the multistage rectangles are built around the *subscripts* of the standard normal probability values. These rectangles rocket through space across the sampling distribution of feasible solutions to the exact optimal in eight minute's time on a Xerox Sigma 6 computer. Lines 160 and 162 store the best answer so far. Line 175 gives us eight intermediate updates on the location of the subscripts and the function value M so far. Lines 190 and 200 give the answer and the probability check of

$$\prod_{i=1}^{5} 2P_i \geqslant 0.80.$$

It seems as though market research, quality control and practicing statisticians could benefit from optimal sample sizes for multiple population sampling under constraints.

Forecasting **6**

A western state has been hard hit by a slump in the home building industry. However, the government is beginning to take sound action to help the economy in general and the housing industry in particular; things have been improving and the housing industry wants to keep them improving.

Specifically, passing Bill A in the state legislature should reduce interest rates and help the housing industry. However, because of considerable opposition to Bill A housing industry lobbyists are marshalling their forces for an all out fight to pass Bill A. They believe that they can show statistically (beyond the shadow of a doubt) that housing starts are a direct function of the prime interest rate (adjusted for a six-month lag).

The figures they have for the past 36 months in the state are given below. Let's prove their point for them with a BASIC program so that they can lobby with some "real" ammunition.

X (prime interest rate six months prior)	Y (number of housing starts in the state per month)
20	800
19	800
18	1000
19.5	780
19	820
18.5	904
19	830
18	900
17.5	1050
17	1200
18	1010
17	1190
16.5	1350
16.5	1400
16.5	1380
16	1600
15.5	1700
15.4	1690
15.25	1710
15	2025
14.75	2250
14.50	2300
15	2280
14.25	2300
14	2500
14	2650
14	2700
14	2680

X	Y
(prime interest rate six months prior)	(number of housing starts in the state per month)
13.5	3080
13.5	3200
13	3310
13	3300
13.5	3310
13	3500
12.5	3500
12.5	4020

The general formula for a straight line is $Y = MX + b$, where M is the slope and b is the Y-intercept. In forecasting and curve fitting theory a straight line is usually written as $Y = \hat{B}_1 X + \hat{B}_0$, where $\hat{B}_1 = (m\Sigma\ XiYi - (\Sigma\ Xi)(\Sigma\ Yi))/(m\Sigma\ X_i^2 - (\Sigma\ Xi)^2)$ and $\hat{B}_0 = \bar{Y} - \hat{B}_1\bar{X}$. These are the "least squares best straight line equations." They produce the unique straight line for any set of (X, Y) ordered pairs such that the sum of the squares of the deviations of the true Y values from the corresponding straight line Y values are a minimum. So in a sense these two equations give us the straight line that is closest to the data.

Let's write a BASIC program to find the best straight line for the housing starts versus the interest data. Then we will test it to see if it is a "good line" (in other words, are the lobbyists right that interest rates are the key?).

```
5    REM FINDING THE LEAST
10   REM SQUARES BEST STRAIGHT
```

```
15    REM LINE FOR HOUSING STARTS
20    REM AS A FUNCTION OF INTEREST RATES
25    DIM X(36), Y(36)
30    S1=0, S2=0, S3=0, S4=0
35    FOR I=1 TO 36
40    READ X(I)
45    NEXT I
50    FOR J=1 TO 36
55    READ Y(J)
60    NEXT J
70    FOR K=1 TO 36
80    S1=S1+X(K)
90    S2=S2+Y(K)
100   S3=S3+X(K)*Y(K)
110   S4=S4+X(K)**2
120   NEXT K
130   B1=(36*S3-S1*S2)/(36*S4-S1**2)
140   B0=(S2/36)-B1*(S1/36)
150   PRINT "SLOPE IS", B1
160   PRINT "Y INTERCEPT IS", B0
165   REM X DATA
170   DATA 20, 19, 18, 19.5, 19, 18.5, 19, 18, 17.5
180   DATA 17, 18, 17, 16.5, 16.5, 16.5, 16, 15.5, 15.4
190   DATA 15.25, 15, 14.75, 14.50, 15, 14.25, 14, 14, 14
200   DATA 14, 13.5, 13.5, 13, 13, 13.5, 13, 12.5, 12.5
205   REM Y DATA
210   DATA 800, 800, 1000, 780, 820, 904
220   DATA 830, 900, 1050, 1200, 1010, 1190
230   DATA 1350, 1400, 1380, 1600, 1700, 1690
240   DATA 1710, 2025, 2250, 2300, 2280, 2300
250   DATA 2500, 2650, 2700, 2680, 3080, 3200
260   DATA 3310, 3300, 3310, 3500, 3500, 4020
270   STOP
280   END
SLOPE IS     -421.900
Y INTERCEPT IS     8607.65
```

From the printout we see that the best straight line for the data is $Y = -421.9X + 8,607.65$. So a 1% drop in the prime interest rate is worth over 400 new housing starts to the western state.

Note: The least squares best straight line equations are derived in many books. See the Suggested Reading section for this and a comparison with L.A.D. and "ridge regression forecasting."

There is an additional question that sometimes should be addressed. The least squares equations for $\hat{B}_0$ and $\hat{B}_1$ will always produce a best straight line regardless of whether or not there is a relationship between the variables represented by the two columns of data. For example, we could take pairs of telephone numbers from the phone book and produce a best straight line even though it would be meaningless. But in our example here, we are pretty sure that there is a strong linear relationship and that the lobbyists are right. Is there a way we could test this statistically? Yes.

What we really want to test is whether or not there is a real slope term B_1 involved in the relationship. If the XY data went around in circles (on a graph), then a horizontal line like $Y = B_0$ or $Y = 0X + B_0$ would represent it adequately. We will test the null hypothesis that the true slope term $B_1 = 0$ versus the alternative that it does not equal zero. We use the formula $Z = (\hat{B}_1 - B_1)/(S/\sqrt{(Xi - \overline{X})^2})$ which is standard normally distributed if we have the right guess for B_1 (namely, zero in this test) and m (the number of ordered pairs) is 32 or more. Therefore, we'll write a BASIC program to calculate Z for our data and straight line. If the Z value is much greater than 3 or less than -3, then we will have observed an event that is almost impossible if $B_1 = 0$. Because we don't believe in impossible events, we will reject $H_0 : B_1 = 0$ (line is not good) and conclude it is good.

Now, in the formula $Z = (\hat{B}_1 - B_1)/(S/\sqrt{(Xi - \overline{X})^2})$ where B_1 is the true slope assumed to be zero, $\hat{B}_1$ is our sample slope calculated from the data and $S = \sqrt{SSE/(m-2)}$, where m is the number of ordered pairs and $SSE = \Sigma(Yi = \overline{Y})^2 - (\hat{B}_1/m)(m \Sigma XiYi - (\Sigma Xi)(\Sigma Yi))$. The program to do these calculations follows:

```
5    REM THEN TEST THE LINE
10   REM TO SEE IF IT IS
15   REM GOOD FOR PREDICTION
20   REM THESE PROGRAMS COULD BE COMBINED
25   DIM X(36), Y(36)
30   S1=0, S2=0, S3=0, S4=0, S5=0, S6=0
35   FOR I=1 TO 36
40   READ X(I)
45   NEXT I
50   FOR J=1TO 36
55   READ Y(J)
60   NEXT J
70   FOR K=1 TO 36
80   S1=S1+X(K)
90   S2=S2+Y(K)
100  S3=S3+X(K)*Y(K)
110  S4=S4+X(K)**2
120  NEXT K
121  M1=S1/36
122  M2=S2/36
123  FOR L=1 TO 36
124  S5=S5+(X(L)-M1)**2
125  S6+S6+(Y(L)-M2)**2
126  NEXT L
127  N1=36*S3-S1*S2
130  B1=(36*S3-S1*S2)/(36*S4-S1**2)
140  S8=SQR((S6-(B1/36)*N1)/34)
150  Z=B1/(S8/SQR(S5))
160  PRINT "Z VALUE IS", Z
165  REM X DATA
```

```
170   DATA 20, 19, 18, 19.5, 19, 18.5, 19, 18, 17.5
180   DATA 17, 18, 17, 16.5, 16.5, 16.5, 16, 15.5, 15.4
190   DATA 15.25, 15, 14.75, 14,50, 15, 14.25, 14, 14, 14
200   DATA 14, 13.5, 13, 5, 13, 13, 13.5, 13, 12.5, 12.5
205   REM Y DATA
210   DATA 800, 800, 1000, 780, 820, 904
220   DATA 830, 900, 1050, 1200, 1010, 1190
230   DATA 1350, 1400, 1480, 1600, 1700, 1690
240   DATA 1710, 2025, 2250, 2300, 2280, 2300
250   DATA 2500, 2650, 2700, 2680, 3080, 3200
260   DATA 3310, 3300, 3310, 3500, 3500, 4020
270   STOP
280   END


Z VALUE IS     -18.8992
```

From the printout we can see that Z is way below -3 ($Z = -18.8992$); therefore, we can confidently reject the null hypothesis that $B_1 = 0$ (line is not good) and conclude that there is a strong negative linear relationship between interest rates and housing starts (six months later). So the lobbyists have their ammunition.

Even after this test there remains the question as to whether the relationship is cause and effect or merely correlation. Here an opinion should suffice. From economics, it seems as though it is cause and effect, i.e., the dropping interest rates directly influence the response variable (the number of housing starts). But even here both variables are probably somewhat correlated to a third variable, economic good times. This does not invalidate the study. Just draw your conclusions with care. Another problem with forecasting problems like this one is, can you predict the future from the recent past? All of this theory presupposes that you can; otherwise the projections are meaningless. If house building is suddenly ruled illegal, then the study can't affect correct action. These types of difficulties occur sometimes with business and economic models and infrequently with scientific models.

The other factor here is that you may have the correct forecast and you can't get anyone to believe it or act on it. As an example, the author read in the grade school *Weekly Reader* newspaper in the late 1950s that a petroleum engineer had done a forecasting study and had concluded that if the United States and the rest of the world continued their present (1950s, that is) increase in use of oil and their present oil policies, that the world would begin to have an oil shortage in the 1970s and 1980s. To say this engineer was correct is one of the twentieth century's great understatements. But the problem was that few people acted on his wisdom.

Another point here is the difference between a cause and effect relationship and one that is just showing high correlation. The housing starts versus prime interest rates certainly has many elements of the cause and effect relationship. Let's look at two variables that are highly correlated, but not related in a cause and effect way.

The X variable is an individual's score on a golf aptitude test designed by the author. The score is a weighted sum (total) of a person's performance in eight categories:

1) Ability to play ping pong
2) Ability to shoot pool
3) Ability to shoot baskets in basketball
4) Patience
5) Competitiveness
6) Ability to concentrate
7) Strong legs
8) Love of outdoors

The Y variable is how good a golfer the test taker is or becomes (can be measured numerically by the person's golf scores).

Now if 32 or more people are tested with X and Y (if they play golf) or tested with X and trained in Y (if they are beginners in golf), the least squares best straight line will be a good fit for the data. The Z test will give a value far away from zero, indicating a strong relationship between X and Y. But the relationship is correlative and not cause and effect. The correlation can be very useful for advising people on hobbies and sports, etc., and it can identify a certain potentially good athlete. But that's it. It's not cause and effect, because, if it were, then the way to improve at golf would be to keep taking the X golf aptitude test over and over again instead of playing golf and getting professional instruction (the real way to get better at golf).

Correlation can be useful and so can cause and affect, but don't mix them up.

One final point. $Z = (\hat{B}_1 - B_1)/(S/\sqrt{(Xi - \overline{X})^2})$ is standard normally distributed if $m \geqslant 32$, as stated before. But if $m < 32$ (m is the number of ordered pairs), then the same formula is t distributed (like the normal curve only more spread out). $t = (\hat{B}_1 - B_1)/(S/\sqrt{(Xi - \overline{X})^2})$. So forecasting tests can still be done if the sample sizes are small.

Small-Sample Problems 7

Student's t distribution is used for a variety of small-sample (usually something less than 30 samples) problems. The formula for the t– distribution is

$$f(x) = \frac{\Gamma\left(\dfrac{K+1}{2}\right)}{\sqrt{K\pi}\ \Gamma\left(\dfrac{K}{2}\right)\left(1 + \dfrac{X^2}{K}\right)^{(K+1)/2}}$$

for $-\infty < X < +\infty$, where Γ is the gamma function and $\Gamma(r)$ = $\int_0^\infty X^{r-1}\ e^{-x} dx$ and K is a parameter called degrees of freedom. K varies from 1 to 2 to 3 to 29 as there are 29 different t distributions all centered at zero and all completely symmetric about zero. When $K = 1$ the distribution is flatter and more spread out than when $K = 2$. The t curve with $K = 2$ is flatter and more spread out than when $K = 3$, and so on until the t curve converges to the standard normal curve when $K > 30$.

The Boulder Pass Quality Control Associates have been given seven new model cars to drive all over the country until their engines give out. They want to see if the engines in the new model cars will last longer than the ones in the old model cars. The car company involved, the Okemos Car Company, would like to make this claim, but they want an independent tester like Boulder Pass to drive the cars so the results will be more credible.

The mean on the old cars was 120,000 miles. The results of the test on the new cars are 139, 141, 119, 163, 150, 148 and 155 in thousands of miles. Write a BASIC program to test to see if $H_0 : \mu = 120$ versus $H_A : \mu \neq 120$ at the $\alpha = 0.01$ (only take a 1% chance of being wrong if they reject the null hypothesis). It turns out that $t = (\overline{X} - \mu)/(S/\sqrt{M})$ is t distributed with $K = M - 1$ degrees of freedom if the distribution sampled is approximately normally distributed. (We assume here that life of car distances are normally distributed.)

Similar to our normal curve integrals we can integrate the t density for $K = 6$ degrees of freedom to find the upper and lower 0.005 points for the test. In this case they are ±3.707. The program to do the calculations follows:

```
2    REM THE OKEMOS CAR COMPANY
3    REM HAS BOULDER PASS PERFORM A
5    REM T TEST TO TEST TO SEE IF THE
15   REM NEW MODEL CAR LASTS LONGER
30   REM MEAN LIFE OF 120,000 MILES
35   DIM X(7)
40   S1=0, S2=0
45   FOR I=1 TO 7
50   READ X(I)
55   NEXT I
60   FOR K=1 TO 7
65   S1=S1+S(K)
70   NEXT K
75   M=S1/7
80   FOR L=1 TO 7
```

```
90   S2=S2+(X(L)-M)**2
100  NEXT L
110  S=SQR(S2/6)
120  T=(M-120)/(S/SQR(7))
130  PRINT 'CALCULATED T VALUE IS', T
140  DATA 139, 141, 119, 163, 150, 148, 155
150  STOP
160  END
```

The printout is:

CALCULATED T VALUE IS   4.704596

This is comfortably outside the ±3.707 upper and lower ½%
t values for six degrees of freedom. Therefore, Boulder Pass
can conclude that the mean length of life of these new model
cars is much longer than the mean length of life of last year's
model. Okemos Car Company can assert correctly, with no
fear of the government taking them to court, that their new
model cars last longer.

As an exercise find the integrals of the t distribution

$$t = \frac{\Gamma\left(\frac{K+1}{2}\right)}{\sqrt{K\pi}\,\Gamma\left(\frac{K}{2}\right)\left(1 + \frac{X^2}{K}\right)^{(K+1)/2}}$$

for $K = 6$ degrees of freedom to produce the upper and lower
½% values.

Note that if M had been 30 or more Boulder Pass could
have used the standard normal test $Z = (\overline{X} - \mu)/(S/\sqrt{M})$. But
with each car costing $5,000 to deliver to Boulder Pass, the
test would have been prohibitively expensive.

This is why business people and scientists prefer small-sample t tests when each sample value is expensive to obtain and/or the test destroys the sample, as in this case.

The Okemos Car Company executives are delighted with the results of the test. This will help their advertising campaign a lot. However, they would also like to prove that their same new model has a longer car life than their top competitor's similar entry into the market. They again hire Boulder Pass, and give them the money to go out and buy five of Okemos Car's new model and five of their competitor's new model. Then Boulder Pass drives them until they quit and records the mileage as below:

Okemos Car (mileage in thousands of miles)	Competition's Car (mileage in thousands of miles)
136	129
147	116
151 $\bar{X}_1 = 142.8$	138 $\bar{X}_2 = 126.8$
137	141
143	110

Will the Okemos Car Company executives be happy at the α = 0.05 level?

We have a two-sample test for means for large samples. There exists a corresponding small sample two-sample t test for means:

$$t = ((\bar{X}_1 - \bar{X}_2) - (\mu_1 - \mu_2))/\sqrt{S^2/M_1 + S^2/M_2}$$

is t distributed with $M_1 + M_2 - 2$ degrees of freedom if the samples were taken from two approximately normal distributions with about the same variability. Also, S^2 is the so-called pooled variance $S^2 = ((M_1 - 1)S_1^2 + (M_2 - 1)S_2^2)/(M_1 + M_2 - 2)$.

Assuming length-of-car-life mileages are normally distributed with similar variability in the two distributions, let's write a BASIC program to do the *t* formula calculations (the Boulder Pass experiment). From integrating the *t* density we get the upper and lower $t0.025$ points to be ± 2.306. This means that if $H_0 : \mu_1 = \mu_2$ as hypothesized, the calculated t value stands a 95% chance of landing between ± 2.306. On the other hand, if it lands outside ± 2.306, we can reject that $\mu_1 = \mu_2$ (cars are the same) with taking only a 5% chance of being wrong. The program follows:

```
5    REM TWO SAMPLE T TEST
10   REM TO TEST OKEMOS CAR
15   REM LIFE AGAINST THE COMPETITION
20   DIM X(5), Y(5)
30   T1=0, T2=0, T3=0, T4=0
40   FOR I=1 TO 5
50   READ X(I)
60   T1=T1+X(I)
70   NEXT I
80   FOR J=1 TO 5
90   READ Y(J)
100  T2-T2+Y(J)
110  NEXT J
120  M1=T1/5
130  M2=T2/5
140  FOR K=1 TO 5
150  T3=T3+(X(K)-M1)**2
160  T4=T4+(Y(K)-M2)**2
170  NEXT K
180  T3=T3/4
190  T4=T4/4
200  S2=(4*T3+4*T4)/8
210  T=(M1-M2)/SQR(S2/5+S2/5)
220  REM X DATA OKEMOS CAR
230  DATA 136, 147, 151, 137, 143
240  REM Y DATA COMPETITION
```

```
250  DATA 129, 116, 138, 141, 110
260  PRINT "T VALUE IS", T
270  STOP
280  END
```

The printout is:

    T VALUE IS   2.390991

Therefore, we reject the equality of the cars (just barely at the 5% level).

Exercises to Part I

1. Write a BASIC program to sort the following 100 numbers and print them from largest to smallest:

242	542	503	493	138
371	831	708	221	259
752	819	821	75	305
788	797	450	169	772
738	298	509	314	852
215	576	78	285	395
143	771	886	413	412
428	52	604	752	552
263	49	32	813	666
362	645	707	95	852
630	699	499	47	900
374	64	250	38	340
777	518	169	188	836
852	807	106	95	952
862	945	55	89	355
628	706	12	97	106
285	323	977	195	333
542	318	947	856	550
420	325	921	830	230
857	528	812	214	445

2. The Carolina Key Group Ltd. has five production lines that they would like to test to see if they are producing product KCR5 at the same level of quality. The number of defects per day from each production line is given for a random 10-day period. They are:

Production Line 1	Production Line 2	Production Line 3	Production Line 4	Production Line 5
18	17	41	52	2
62	19	25	46	3
59	27	29	12	10
48	23	42	28	16
73	20	43	51	35
63	14	50	55	68
72	7	49	57	5
80	31	37	58	6
89	32	30	61	8
83	13	26	60	9

Is there a real difference in quality at the $a = 0.05$ level? The company decides to test H_0 :no difference versus H_A a difference in quality by using the nonparametric Kruskal-Wallis test

$$H = \frac{12}{M(M+1)} \left(\Sigma \frac{R_i{}^2}{M_i} \right) - 3(M+1),$$

where M is the total number of readings (50 in this case) and R_i is the rank sum of each column. (The 50 numbers must be ranked from 1 to 50, and the rankings for each column are summed yielding R_1, R_2, R_3, R_4 and R_5.) Then if H_0 is true, H is chi square distributed with the number of populations minus one degree of freedom. The chi square distribution formula is:

$$f(x) = \begin{cases} \dfrac{1}{2^{m/2}\, \Gamma(m/2)} X^{m/2-1} e^{-x/2}, & 0 \leqslant X < \infty \\ 0 & \text{if } X < 0 \end{cases}$$

where m is the number of degrees of freedom. Therefore, solve the problem for Carolina Key by writing BASIC programs to sort the 50 numbers, then integrate the gamma (Γ) function to determine $\Gamma(2)$. Then write a BASIC program to integrate the chi square distribution for four degrees of freedom to determine the upper 5% point. Finally, write a BASIC program to do the H calculations to answer Carolina Key's question.

3. Set up a FOR NEXT BASIC integration loop to produce a chart of the gamma function values ($\Gamma(K)$) for $K = 0.5$, $1, 1.5, 2, 2.5, \ldots, 15$.

4. How large a sample should a market researcher draw in order to be 95% sure that the sample proportion he or she obtains is within 0.02 of the true but unknown proportion for his or her product's market share?

5. How large a sample should a quality control engineer draw in order to estimate the mean length of a bolt to within 0.09 inches with 98% confidence if the standard deviation S is known to be 0.3?

6. Find the least squares best straight line for the data below:

X	Y
1	2
1	3
2	4
2	3

Then test at the $a = 0.10$ level to see if the line is good.

7. Do a t test to test for a difference in the mean $\mu = 14$ sales per day from the new group at the $\alpha = 0.05$ level if the six new sales people sold 18, 19, 31, 12, 17 and 35 on the first day.

8. Do a Kruskal-Wallis test to test for a difference in quality among three production lines, A, B and C, if their number of defectives per day for five days is as below. Test at the $a = 0.05$ level.

A	B	C
19	20	29
16	23	31
14	28	33
21	18	32
10	30	27

9. Two production lines are being tested for quality. A sample of 1,000 parts yields 10 defectives in production line A. A sample of 1,000 of the same parts in line B yields 30 defectives. Is there a real difference in quality here at the $\alpha = 0.05$ level?

    Note that

    $$Z = ((P_1 - P_2) - (\pi_1 - \pi_2))/\sqrt{P(1 - P)/M_1 + P(1 - P)/M_2}$$

    is standard normally distributed if $M_1 + M_2 > 30$. P is the pooled proportion of both populations.

10. How large a sample should a market researcher draw in order to be 99% sure that the sample proportion obtained is within 0.03 of the true but unknown proportion for the product's market share?

11. How large a sample should a quality control engineer draw in order to estimate the mean length of a steel beam to within 0.08 inches with 95% confidence if the standard deviation S is known to be 0.4?

12. Two production lines are supposedly exactly the same. However, $M_1 = 20$ sample days in production line 1 yielded an average daily production of $\overline{X}_1 = 103$ units with $S_1 = 5$.

M_2 = 20 sample days in production line 2 yielded an average daily production of $\bar{X}_2$ = 114 units with S_2 = 4. Is there a real difference at the a = 0.05 level?

13. Find the least squares best straight line for the following data:

X	Y
1	1
3	2
2	6

14. Two sales training programs are compared. M_1 = 25 salespersons from program 1 sold an average of $\bar{X}_1$ = 62 units a week with S_1 = 8. M_2 = 15 salespersons from program 2 sold an average of $\bar{X}_2$ = 59 units a week with S_1 = 7. Is there a real difference at the α = 0.10 level?

15. Your supplier guarantees a 0.03 defective rate. You sample 1,000 products and notice 63 defectives. Is your supplier treating you honestly at the α = 0.05 level? Do a one-sided test.

16. A sample of the next 100 customers to use four checkout lanes revealed M_1 = 20 in the first line, M_2 = 30 in the second line, M_3 = 10 in the third and M_4 = 40 in the fourth. Are the lines being used equally? Test at the α = 0.05 level. Test the hypothesis that $H_0: \pi_1 = \pi_2 = \pi_3 = \pi_4 = 0.25$ versus the alternative that H_0 is untrue by using the Pearson chi square test

$$\chi^2 = \Sigma \frac{(M_i - M\pi_i)^2}{M\pi_i}$$

where $M = M_1 + M_2 + M_3 + M_4$. This formula is chi square distributed with the number of classifications minus one degree of freedom. Write a BASIC program to do the calculations and integrate the chi square function for three degrees of freedom to find the upper 0.05 point needed for the test.

17. Write a BASIC program to create a chart of the upper 0.10, 0.05, 0.025, 0.01 and 0.005 points for the 29 different t distributions (for $K = 1, 2, 3, \ldots, 29$ degrees of freedom).

18. Create a random number generator from RND(X) that produces standard normally distributed random numbers.

19. Write a BASIC program to test the normally distributed random number generator from exercise 18 with the Pearson chi square test to see if the numbers are really coming out normally distributed.

20. The Castle Guard Company has the following data relating market share to level of advertising:

X (amount of advertising in $10,000/year)	Y (percentage of market share)
5	10
8	12
9	14
10	16
12	17
14	18
16	21

Write a BASIC program to find the least squares best straight line for the data. Also write a BASIC program to

find the least absolute deviation (L.A.D.) best straight line.
(The L.A.D. line is found by minimizing

$$\sum_{i=1}^{7} | Yi - \hat{B}_0 + \hat{B}_1 X_i |$$

as a function of $\hat{B}_0$ and $\hat{B}_1$.) Compare the two lines; they
should be close.

21. Write a BASIC program to calculate and print $M!$ for M
= 1, 2, 3, . . . , 15. ($M!$ is read M factorial.) Compare the
printout with the gamma function printout for exercise 3.

PART II

Futuristic Problems

Comparison of BASIC and FORTRAN

8

Many people like to learn FORTRAN after learning BASIC. FORTRAN is a very popular and powerful computer language. It is so similar to BASIC that with a few pages of comparison it will be easy to pick up.

FORTRAN is like BASIC in that statements are written vertically on a page and operated on sequentially from top to bottom unless interrupted by a logical command that calls for a computer decision.

In BASIC all lines must be numbered. In FORTRAN lines don't have to be numbered. A line is numbered only if it is possible to branch to it in some fashion. These line numbers are placed in columns 1 through 5. Stay out of column 6. The actual statements should start in column 7.

REM stands for a comment statement in BASIC. A *C* typed in column 1 reserves that line for comments in FORTRAN.

Variables in FORTRAN can be any sequence of up to six letters, numbers and $ symbols as long as they don't start with a number. Any variables starting with the letters *I* through *N* are integer variables and they truncate any fractional part of a number ($I = 14.4$ yields $I = 14$, whereas $X = 14.4$ yields $X = 14.4$, as an example). Any other variables are regular real variables.

INTEGER X, Y, Z changes the named variables to integer variables. And REAL I, IK, J changes these integer variables to reals.

Just as DIM X(100) declares the 100-variable array in **BASIC**, DIMENSION X(100) accomplishes similar things in FORTRAN. Generally, seven places of accuracy are carried and printed in FORTRAN. If that isn't enough, the statement DOUBLE PRECISION X(100), K, AZ1, etc., would let these variables carry about 14 places of accuracy.

PRINT in BASIC is usually replaced by WRITE in FOR-TRAN for printing. (Note that PRINT is used in some versions of FORTRAN.) READ is READ in FORTRAN.

In logical statements in FORTRAN

.GT.	is greater than
.LT.	is less than
.GE.	is greater than or equal
.LE.	is less than or equal
.EQ.	is equal
.NE.	is not equal
.OR.	is or
.AND.	is and

The symbols =, +, -, /, *, ** and ( ) have the same meanings and uses in FORTRAN as in BASIC.

IF THEN in BASIC is replaced by IF(a) S where if what is in parentheses is true, command S is followed (the THEN is implied). And if (a) is false, the next statement is executed.

GO TO 5 in BASIC is GO TO 5 in FORTRAN, except that it can also be attached to a logical IF as in IF(X.LT.Y) GO TO 15, etc., giving two-way control. The arithmetic IF (there are two IF commands in FORTRAN) of the form IF(X)5, 6, 7, for example, tells the computer to go to the line numbered 5 if X is negative, to line numbered 6 if X is zero and to the line numbered 7 if X is positive.

And of course the powerful *FOR NEXT* looping statements in BASIC are replaced in FORTRAN by the powerful *DO* loops which make all problems solvable. A few examples:

BASIC	*FORTRAN Equivalent*

```
5   FOR X=1 TO 100        DO 1 I=1, 100
10
15
20  NEXT X                1 CONTINUE
```

You must use an integer variable for the "index" of the *DO* loop.

```
5   FOR J=18 TO 600 STEP 2   DO 16 J=18, 600, 2
10
15
20  NEXT J                   16 CONTINUE

                             INTEGER X, Y
5   FOR X=1 TO 50            DO 12 X=1, 50
10  FOR Y=1 TO 60            DO 12 Y=1, 60
15
20
30
40  NEXT Y
50  NEXT X                   12 CONTINUE
```

or

```
INTEGER X, Y
DO 12 X=1, 50
DO 42 Y=1, 60

42 CONTINUE
12 CONTINUE
```

The order of computer execution in nested *DO* loops is the same as in nested *FOR NEXT* statements. You can branch *out* of a *DO* loop anytime, but as in BASIC, don't branch *into* a loop. Enter it from the starting controlling *DO* statement.

```
                          INTEGER X, R, T, Z
5    FOR X=Z TO R STEP T  DO 10 X=Z, R, T
10
15   NEXT X               10 CONTINUE
```

As long as Z, R and T have values before arriving at the *DO* 10 line.

Wrong   *Wrong*

```
                          INTEGER X, Y
FOR X=1 to 80             DO 20 X=1, 80
FOR Y=11 TO 70            DO 25 Y=1, 70

NEXT X                    20 CONTINUE
NEXT Y                    25 CONTINUE
```

Don't cross loops.

There isn't any standard random number generator in FORTRAN, but many are available for use. Dudewicz's book on the subject of random number generators could be of help (see Suggested Reading).

ABS( ) is absolute value and *DABS( )* is double precision absolute value. Similarly for trignometric functions.

A Function with 9
Eighty Thousand Terms

A 20,000-variable nonlinear system of equations is stated and a 64-statement multistage Monte Carlo FORTRAN program is written to solve it. Several of the solutions are accurate to at least ten places in all 20,000 variables.

____THE PROBLEM

Find several solutions accurate to at least ten decimal places in all 20,000 variables to the following system of equations

$$\sum_{i=1}^{19{,}998} (X_i^2 + 2X_{i+1})X_{i+2} = 90{,}000$$

$$\sum_{i=1}^{19{,}998} X_i X_{i+1} X_{1+2} = 81{,}000$$

$$\sum_{i=1}^{20{,}000} X_i^3 = 80{,}000$$

subject to $-100 \leqslant X_i \leqslant 100$ for $i = 1, 2, 3, \ldots, 20{,}000$.

We transform this problem to minimize the 80,000-term function

$$f(X_1, X_2, X_3, \ldots, X_{20,000})$$

$$= \left| \sum_{i=1}^{19,998} (X_i^2 + 2X_{i+1})X_{i+2} - 90,000 \right|$$

$$+ \left| \sum_{i=1}^{19,998} X_i X_{i+1} X_{i+2} - 81,000 \right| + \left| \sum_{i=1}^{29,000} X_i^3 - 80,000 \right|$$

subject to $-100 \leqslant X_i \leqslant 100$ for $i = 1, 2, 3, \ldots, 20,000$, and solve it using multistage. The FORTRAN IV program (run on a very large computer) is below along with the solutions and an explanation of the program.

```
C      MULTI STAGE MONTE CARLO
C      DOUBLE PRECISION SOLUTION TO A
C      TWENTY THOUSAND VARIABLE
C      NONLINEAR PROBLEM
       DOUBLE PRECISION P, P1, P2, P3, M, AU, YFL, L
       DOUBLE PRECISION X(20000), A(20000)
       INTEGER Z
       DOUBLE PRECISION V(10)
       WRITE (3, 303)
 303   FORMAT ('1', T1, 'MULTI STAGE MONTE CARLO
                       SOLUTIONS')
       WRITE (3, 304)
 304   FORMAT ('0')
       IX=8354613
       DO 75 IB=1, 10
       F=3.00
       DO 1 I=1, 20000
 1     A(I)=0.0
       M=1.0 E70
       DO 19 J=1, 40
       Z=20
```

```
        DO 32 I=1, Z
        DO 4 K=1, 20000
        IF (A(K)-100.0/F**J.LT.-100.0) GO TO 50
        GO TO 60
50      L=-100.0
        GO TO 65
60      L=A(K)-100.0/F**J
65      IF (A(K)+100.0/F**J.GT.100.0) GO TO 80
        GO TO 90
80      AU=100.0-L
        GO TO 100
90      AU=A(K)+100.0/F**J L
100     CONTINUE
        IY=IX*65539
        IF(IY)5, 6, 6
5       IY=IY+2147483647+1
6       YFL=IY
        YFL=YFL*.4656613E-9
        X(K)=L+YFL*AU
        IX=IY
4       CONTINUE
        P1=0.0
        DO 666 IT=1,19998
666     P1=P1+(X(IT)**2+2*X(IT+1))*X(IT+2)
        P1=DABS(P1-90000.0)
        P2=0.0
        DO 667 IS=1, 19998
667     P2=P2+X(IS)*X(IS+1)*X(IS+2)
        P2=DABS(P2-81000.0)
        P3=0.0
        DO 669 IK=1, 20000
669     P3=P3+X(IK)**3
        P3=DABS(P3-80000.0)
        P=P1+P2+P3
        IF(P.LT.M) GO TO 200
        GO TO 32
```

```
200   M=P
      DO 11 I1=1, 20000
      A(I1)=X(I1)
11    CONTINUE
32    CONTINUE
19    CONTINUE
      V(IB)=M
      WRITE (3, 302)M
302   FORMAT ('  ', F20.12)
75    CONTINUE
      STOP
      END
```

BASIC Version

```
2     REM TRANSLATION OF PRECEDING
3     REM TWENTY THOUSAND VARIABLE
4     REM PROBLEM WITH SEVEN PLACE
5     REM ANSWERS PRINTED
6     REM YOU NEED A LOT OF COMPUTER
7     REM TIME FOR THIS ONE
10    DIM X(20000), A(20000)
11    X=1
12    F=3
14    FOR I2=1 TO 20000
16    A(I2)=0.0
17    NEXT I2
18    M=1.0 E60
20    FOR J=1 TO 40
24    Z=20
26    FOR I=1TO Z
28    FOR K=1 TO 20000
30    IF A(K)-100.0/F**J < -100.0 THEN 50
40    GO TO 60
50    L=-100.0
```

```
55    GO TO 65
60    L=A(K)-100.0/F**J
65    IF A(K)+100.0/F**J > 100.0 THEN 80
70    GO TO 90
80    U=100.0-L
85    GO TO 100
90    U=A(K)+100.0/F**J-L
100   X(K)=L+RND(X)*U
102   NEXT K
103   P1=0.0
104   FOR IT=1 TO 19998
105   P1=P1+(X(IT)**2+2*X(IT+1))*X(IT⏋2)
106   P1=ABS(P1-90000.0)
107   NEXT IT
108   P2=0.0
109   FOR IS=1 TO 19998
110   P2=P2+X(IS)*X(IS+1)*X(IS+2)
111   P2=ABS(P2-81000.0)
112   NEXT IS
113   P3=0.0
114   FOR IK=1 TO 20000
115   P3=P3+X(IK)**3
116   P3=ABS(P3-80000.0)
117   NEXI IK
118   P=P1+P2+P3
120   IF P < M THEN 160
130   GO TO 170
160   FOR I1=1 TO 20000
162   A(I1)=XI(1)
165   NEXT I1
168   M=P
170   NEXT I
180   NEXT J
190   PRINT M
200   STOP
210   END
```

Multistage Monte Carlo Solutions

494.662327918079	local optimal
0.000020115782	solution
16534.641334433920	local optimal
0.000003353503	solution
118373.674560192200	local optimal
1147.748653182803	local optimal
1193611.524768268000	local optimal
3020.722505937563	local optimal
8436.802628791993	local optimal

The program drew 20 × 40 = 800 sample answers nine times and produced two solutions and seven local optimals. (Note that it should have drawn ten sets of 800, but the program was stopped after nine due to time limitations on that day.) To improve performance we changed the line 0016 Z=20 to 0016 Z=40 and reran the program drawing 40 × 40 = 1,600 sample answers each time. The error terms are below. We produced nine very accurate solutions and one local optimal.*

Multistage Monte Carlo Solutions

0.000000001965	solution
0.000000003725	solution
0.000000001863	solution
0.000000012442	solution
217.374948320517	local optimal
0.000000012733	solution
0.000000007974	solution
0.000000002707	solution
0.000000004788	solution
0.000000119253	solution

---

*The Z=40 run which produced nine solutions took 32 hours, 42 minutes and 39 seconds on a very large and fast computer.

The individual variable values for the solutions are stored in the 20,000-dimensional A variable and can be printed as desired. This was omitted to save space.

____EXPLANATION OF THE PROGRAM

Every optimization problem has a sampling distribution of feasible solutions. Usually these sampling distributions mark off clear-cut trails to the optimal (or an optimal) solution to the problem in question. Figure 9.1 partially illustrates this phenomenon and the n-dimensional rectangles of decreasing size (in a multistage program) tracking and finding a solution. (See the Suggested Reading section for more examples.)

A multistage program is divided into sections: initial statements, loops, rectangles, function, comparison, storage and printing statements. Lines 1 through 8 (0001 through 0008) are initial statements that declare variables to be double precision and set up a heading and storage. Line 9 is the first value for the random number generator which is in lines 30 through 34. The number in line 9 should be changed in each run so that a different "random" sequence is produced each time. Line 10 sets up a loop to look for ten solutions. Line 11 specifies the focusing factor (in this case $F=3$). Lines 12 and 13 center the first 20,000-dimensional rectangle at $(0, 0, 0, \ldots, 0)$. Line 14 initializes the M variable (which will store the function value or error term) to be an artifically large number so that the first time line 51 is encountered P will be less than M and the first real feasible solution will be stored.

Line 15 says that there will be 39 reductions in rectangle sizes (after the initial size when $J=1$). Line 16 allows 20 sample answers to be drawn inside the reduced rectangle region in question each time. The DO 32 loop in line 17 produces the 20 sample answers each time it's encountered. The DO 4

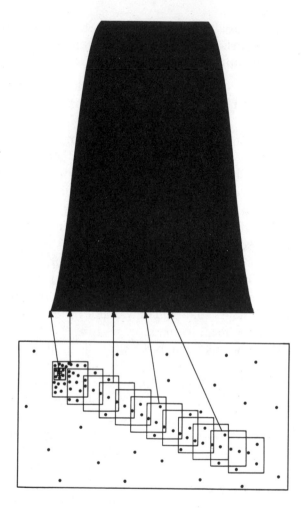

FIGURE 9.1 MINIMIZING WITH RECTANGLES.

loop in line 18 reads in a random coordinate for each of the 20,000 variables. Hence, one complete loop of DO 4 constitutes producing one of the 800 feasible solutions in this multistage run. Note that the random variable value is stored in YFL.

The transformed function is evaluated in lines 38 through 50. Line 51 checks to see if this feasible solution is less than the best (smallest in this case) so far. If it is, it is stored in the storage space in lines 52 through 56. Then the process repeats itself 799 times and by then it is hoped the function value is zero.

The key to any multistage program is the DO 4 loop that controls the rectangles and the sampling. The IF statements in there make sure that samples are not read in outside the bounds of the rectangle in question. Also, the rectangles are centered about the best answer so far and repositioned as better answers appear in the process.

Many-Body Problems $\mathbf{10}$

The Star Walker Space Corporation plans to launch five space probes during the coming year. They will be launched separately at different times from five different 1, 2, 3 coordinate points in the solar system. Their equations of motion for the year are given below as a function of seconds after launch time (X_i for i = 1, 2, 3, 4 and 5):

C_1 = 1,350,000 – 0.2X_1
C_2 = 700,000 – X_1
C_3 = 2,000,000 – 3X_1

D_1 = –15,000,000 + 1.5X_2
D_2 = –24,000,000 + 2.5X_2
D_3 = –33,500,000 + 3.5X_2

E_1 = –20,010,000 + 0.4X_3
E_2 = 15,258,000 – 3X_3
E_3 = –24,992,000 + 0.5X_3

$$F_1 = 160,000,000 - 8X_4$$
$$F_2 = -179,912,000 + 0.9X_4$$
$$F_3 = 200,000,450 - 10X_4$$

$$G_1 = -60,000,000 + 5X_5$$
$$G_2 = -71,889,900 + 6X_5$$
$$G_3 = 85,000,000 - 7X_5$$

For example, C_1 is the first dimension coordinate point for rocket 1. F_3 is the third dimension coordinate point for rocket 4, etc.

Each of the five rockets has a number of tasks to perform throughout the flights. However, a few important measurements and observations must be taken when rocket 1 is close to rocket 2, and rocket 2 is close to rocket 3, and rocket 3 is close to 4 and 4 is close to 5. This must happen simultaneously.

So our problem is, in the next year (31,536,000 seconds) when should we launch each rocket so that the total distance from rockets 1 to 2 to 3 to 4 to 5 is a minimum at some point during the coming year (versus all other launch combinations)? Therefore, we have minimize

$$D = \sqrt{(C_1 - D_1)^2 + (C_2 - D_2)^2 + (C_3 - D_3)^2}$$
$$+ \sqrt{(D_1 - E_1)^2 + (D_2 - E_2)^2 + (D_3 - E_3)^2}$$
$$+ \sqrt{(E_1 - F_1)^2 + (E_2 - F_2)^2 + (E_3 - F_3)^2}$$
$$+ \sqrt{(F_1 - G_1)^2 + (F_2 - G_2)^2 + (F_3 - G_3)^2}$$

subject to $0 \leqslant X_i \leqslant 31,536,000$ seconds (one year) for $i = 1$, 2, 3, 4 and 5.

The multistage Monte Carlo minimization program to find 20 solutions to this problem follows. Note that the 20 solutions in the printout are all the same. This is the true optimal.

The five-dimensional rectangles in this multistage problem did not have any trouble tracking the solution through 31,536,-001[5] answers and finding it. Only 42,000 total sample answers had to be drawn.

```
1.000   C    MANY BODY PROBLEM
2.000   C    WITH FIVE ROCKETS
3.000        INTEGER Z
4.000        DOUBLE PRECISION X(5), B(5), M, U, PF
5.000        DOUBLE PRECISION L(5), N(5), AU(5), A(5)
6.000        DOUBLE PRECISION C1, C2, C3, D1, D2, D3, E1, E2
7.000        DOUBLE PRECISION E3, F1, F2, F3, G1, G2, G3
8.000        DOUBLE PRECISION H1, H2, H3, H4
9.000        INPUT IY
10.000       DO 75 IB=1, 20
11.000       F=2
12.000       DO 1 I=1, 5
13.000       B(I)=0.0
14.000       A(I)=15768000.
15.000  1    N(I)=31536000.
16.000       M=1.0 E70
17.000       DO 19 J=1, 42
18.000       Z=1000
19.000       DO 3 I=1, Z
20.000       DO 4 K=1, 5
21.000       IF (A(K)-N(K)/F**J.LT.B(K)) GO TO 50
22.000       GO TO 60
23.000  50   L(K)=B(K)
24.000       GO TO 65
25.000  60   L(K)=A(K)-N(K)/F**J
26.000  65   IF (A(K)+N(K)/F**J.GT.N(K)) GO TO 80
27.000       GO TO 90
28.000  80   AU(K)=N(K)-L(K)
29.000       GO TO 100
30.000  90   AU(K)=A(K)+N(K)/F**J-L(K)
```

```
31.000  100  CALL RANDOM (IY, JY, U)
32.000       X(K)=L(K)+U*AU(K)
33.000       IY=JY
34.000  4    CONTINUE
35.000       C1=1350000.-2*X(1)
36.000       C2=700000.-X(1)
37.000       C3=2000000.-3*X(1)
38.000       D1=-15000000.+1.5*X(2)
39.000       D2=-24000000.+2.5*X(2)
40.000       D3=-33500000.+3.5*X(2)
41.000       E1=-20010000.+.4*X(3)
42.000       E2=15258000.-3*X(3)
43.000       E3=-24992000.+.5*X(3)
44.000       F1=160000000.-8*X(4)
45.000       F2=-179912000.+.9*X(4)
46.000       F3=200000450.-10*X(4)
47.000       G1=-60000000.+5*X(5)
48.000       G2=-71889900+6*X(5)
49.000       G3=85000000.-7*X(5)
50.000       H1=((C1-D1)**2+(C2-D2)**2+(C3-D3)**2)**.5
51.000       H2=((D1-E1)**2+(D2-E2)**2+(D3-E3)**2)**.5
52.000       H3=((E1-F1)**2+(E2-F2)**2+(E3-F3)**2)**.5
53.000       H4=((F1-G1)**2+(F2-G2)**2+(F3-G3)**2)**.5
54.000       PF=H1+H2+H3+H4
55.000       IF(PF.LT.M) GO TO 200
56.000       GO TO 3
57.000  200  CONTINUE
58.000       M=PF
59.000       DO 11 I1=1, 5
60.000       A(I1)=X(I1)
61.000  11   CONTINUE
62.000  3    CONTINUE
63.000       IF(J.EQ.42) GO TO 662
64.000       GO TO 19
```

```
65.000  662  CONTINUE
66.000       WRITE (108, 300)A(1), A(2), A(3), A(4), A(5)
67.000  300  FORMAT (' ', 5F14.2)
68.000       WRITE (108, 302)M
69.000  302  FORMAT (' ', F20.12)
70.000  19   CONTINUE
71.000  75   CONTINUE
72.000       STOP
73.000       END


2    REM BASIC TRANSLATION OF
3    REM PRECEDING FIVE ROCKET
4    REM MANY BODY PROBLEM WITH
5    REM SINGLE PRECISION 7 PLACES
6    REM CARRIED FOR SOLUTION
7    DIM A(5), B(5), L(5), N(5), U(5), X(5)
10   F=2
12   M-1.0E30
15   FOR I2=1 TO 5
17   B(I2)=0.0, A(I2)=15768E3, N(I2)=31536E3
18   NEXT I2
20   FOR J=1 TO 38
24   Z=1000
26   FOR I=1 TO Z
28   FOR K=1 TO 5
30   IF A(K)-N(K)/F**J < B(K) THEN 50
40   GO TO 60
50   L(K)= B(K)
55   GO TO 65
60   L(K)=A(K)-N(K)/F**J
65   IF A(K)+N(K)/F**J > N(K) THEN 80
70   GO TO 90
80   U(K)=N(K)-L(K)
```

```
85    GO TO 100
90    U(K)=A(K)+N(K)/F**J-L(K)
100   X(K)=L(K)+RND(X)*U(K)
102   NEXT K
103   C1=1350000.-2*X(1)
104   C2=700000.-X(1)
105   C3=2000000.-3*X(1)
106   D1=-15000000.+1.5*X(2)
107   D2=-24000000.+2.5*X(2)
108   D3=-33500000.+3.5*X(2)
109   E1=-20010000.+.4*X(3)
110   E2=15258000.-3*X(3)
111   E3=-24992000.+.5*X(3)
112   F1=160000000.-8*X(4)
113   F2=-179912000.+.9*X(4)
114   F3=200000450.-10*X(4)
115   G1=-60000000.+5*X(5)
116   G2=-71889900+6*X(5)
117   G3=85000000.-7*X(5)
118   H1=((C1-D1)**2+(C2-D2)**2+(C3-D3)**2)**.5
119   H2=((D1-E1)**2+(D2-E2)**2+(D3-E3)**2)**.5
120   H3=((E1-F1)**2+(E2-F2)**2+(E3-F3)**2)**.5
121   H4=((F1-G1)**2+(F2-G2)**2+(F3-G3)**2)**.5
123   P=H1+H2+H3+H4
125   IF P<M THEN 160
130   GO TO 170
160   A(1)=X(1), A(2)=X(2), A(3)=X(3), A(4)=X(4), A(5)=X(5)
162   M=P
170   NEXT I
175   PRINT A(1), A(2), A(3), A(4), A(5)
178   PRINT M
180   NEXT J
190   STOP
200   END
```

The printout from the FORTRAN run is:

```
692724.54 9637616.02 5007464.32 19999113.73 12061725.48
2122272.203931463420
692724.55 9637616.02 5007464.31 19999113.73 12061725.49
2122272.203931463650
692724.56 9637616.02 5007464.31 19999113.73 12061725.48
2122272.203931463650
692724.53 9637616.03 5007464.32 19999113.73 12061725.48
2122272.203931465750
692724.54 9637616.02 5007464.31 19999113.73 12061725.48
2122272.203931464350
692724.56 9637616.01 5007464.31 19999113.73 12061725.48
2122272.203931464350
692724.54 9637616.02 5007464.32 19999113.73 12061725.48
2122272.203931462950
692724.55 9637616.02 5007464.32 19999113.73 12061725.48
2122272.203931463650
692724.56 9637616.02 5007464.32 19999113.73 12061725.48
2122272.203931463190
692724.55 9637616.02 5007464.31 19999113.73 12061725.48
2122272.203931463190
692724.55 9637616.02 5007464.31 19999113.73 12061725.48
2122272.203931463650
692724.55 9637616.02 5007464.31 19999113.73 12061725.48
2122272.203931463650
692724.55 9637616.02 5007464.31 19999113.73 12061725.48
2122272.203931462950
692724.56 9637616.01 5007464.31 19999113.73 12061725.49
2122272.203931465050
692724.55 9637616.02 5007464.31 19999113.73 12061725.48
2122272.203931462950
692724.56 9637616.01 5007464.31 19999113.73 12061725.49
2122272.203931463880
```

692724.56 9637616.01 5007464.31 19999113.73 12061725.49
2122272.203931464820
692724.54 9637616.02 5007464.31 19999113.73 12061725.48
2122272.203931463190
692724.54 9637616.03 5007464.31 19999113.73 12061725.48
2122272.203931464120
692724.55 9637616.02 5007464.31 19999113.73 12061725.48
2122272.203931463190

So

X_1 = 692,724.55 seconds

X_2 = 9,637,616.02 seconds

X_3 = 5,007,464.31 seconds

X_4 = 19,999,113.73 seconds

X_5 = 12,061,725.48 seconds

are the elapsed times when the total minimum distance as specified is reached. Therefore, Star Walker Space Corporation should launch rocket 4 first. Then launch rocket 5 (19,999,-113.73 −12,061,725.48) seconds later. Then launch rocket 2 (12,061,725.48–9,637,616.02) seconds after rocket 5 goes up. Then launch rocket 3 (9,637,616.02 − 5,007,464.31) seconds after launching rocket 2. And lastly, launch rocket 1 (5,007,-464.31–692,724.55) seconds after launching rocket 3.

_____AIR TRAFFIC CONTROL WITH MULTISTAGE

If airports in western Europe handled 5,000 airplanes a day, could the launch times and equations of motion of the planes (subject to crucial safety constraints) be worked out to the satisfaction of all concerned so that there wouldn't be dangerous congestion at the airports or in the skies? It would certainly simplify air traffic controlling if it worked. The problem in chapter 9 demonstrated that some problems with 15–20,000 variables can be solved with multistage. But could a large air traffic network, with all its attendant conditions, be solved and resolved quickly as conditions change? The launch times would also have to be quite reasonable as most airlines like to offer morning, afternoon and evening flights where they have quite a bit of say about takeoff and arrival times. Changing weather and wind speeds and fogged in airports would all necessitate changing and rerunning the model.

This problem might be too difficult for multistage.

Would other large nonlinear networks involving heat, light, resistance, voltage, production or pumping be solvable with multistage? (See the Suggested Reading section.)

A Maximization Problem 11

Figure 11.1 partially illustrates the n-dimensional rectangles in multistage shooting across the feasible solution distribution to the maximum of a function. Figure 11.2 partially illustrates spheres of ever decreasing sizes crossing the feasible solution distribution of

$$P = 26X_1^2 + 77X_2 + 54X_3$$

subject to $0 \leqslant X_i \leqslant 100$ and all X_i's are integers, to find the maximum of $X_1 = X_2 = X_3 = 100$ and $P = 273,100$.

Let's write a multistage Monte Carlo integer program to maximize this function using decreasing size rectangles and drawing only 1,200 total sample answers out of 101^3 possible solutions. The FORTRAN IV program, its corresponding BASIC program equivalent and printout follow figures 11.1 and 11.2.

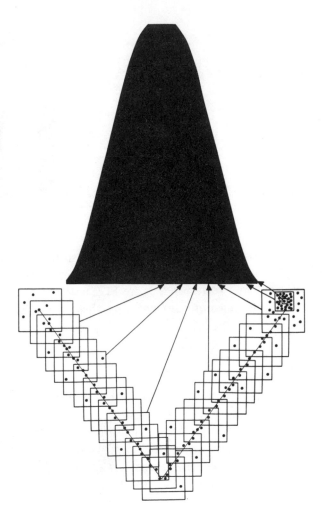

FIGURE 11.1 MAXIMIZING A FUNCTION.

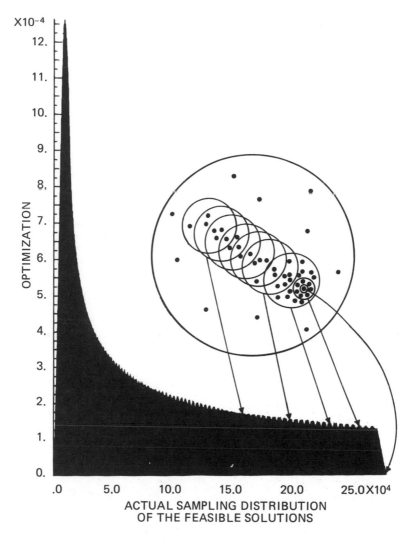

```
1.000    C     MULTI STAGE MONTE CARLO
2.000    C     INTEGER PROGRAM USING CUBES
3.000    C     (INSTEAD OF SPHERES) OF EVER
4.000    C     DECREASING SIZE TO MAXIMIZE P
5.000          DIMENSION N(3), L(3), AU(3)
6.000          INTEGER Z, X(3), A(3), B(3)
7.000          INPUT IY
8.000          M=0
9.000          F=2.0
10.000         DO 1 I=1, 3
11.000         B(I)=0
12.000         A(I)=50
13.000   1     N(I)=100
14.000         DO 19 J=1, 6
15.000         Z=200
15.500         DO 3 I=1, Z
16.000         DO 4 K=1, 3
17.000         IF (A(K)-N(K)/F**J.LT.B(K)) GO TO 50
18.000         GO TO 60
19.000   50    L(K)=B(K)
20.000         GO TO 65
21.000   60    L(K)=A(K)-N(K)/F**J
22.000   65    IF (A(K)+N(K)/F**J.GT.N(K)) GO TO 80
23.000         GO TO 90
24.000   80    AU(K)=N(K)-L(K)
25.000         GO TO 100
26.000   90    AU(K)=A(K)+N(K)/F**J-L(K)
27.000   100   CALL RANDOM (IY, JY, U)
28.000         X(K)=INT(L(K)+U*AU(K)+.5)
29.000         IY=JY
30.000   4     CONTINUE
31.000         P=26*X(1)**2+77*X(2)+54*X(3)
32.000         IF(P.GT.M) GO TO 200
33.000         GO TO 3
34.000   200   M=P
```

```
35.000      A(1)=X(1)
36.000      A(2)=X(2)
37.000      A(3)=X(3)
38.000  3   CONTINUE
39.000  19  CONTINUE
40.000      WRITE (108, 302)A(1), A(2), A(3), M
41.000  302 FORMAT (' ', 4I10)
42.000      STOP
43.000      END
```

```
100         100         100         273100
```

```
5   REM BASIC VERSION OF
6   REM PRECEDING PROGRAM
8   DIM N(3), L(3), U(3), X(3), A(3), B(3), Z
9   F=2
10  X=1
12  M=0
14  FOR I2=1 TO 3
16  B(I2)=0, A(I2)=50, N(I2)=100
18  NEXT I2
20  FOR J=1 TO 6
24  Z=200
26  FOR I=I TO Z
28  FOR K=1 TO 3
30  IF A(K)-N(K)/F**J < B(K) THEN 50
40  GO TO 60
50  L(K)=B(K)
55  GO TO 65
60  L(K)=A(K)-N(K)/F**J
65  IF A(K)+N(K)/F**J > N(K) THEN 80
70  GO TO 90
80  U(K)=N(K)-L(K)
85  GO TO 100
90  U(K)=A(K)+N(K)/F**J-L(K)
```

```
100  X(K)=INT(L(K)+RND(X)*U(K)+.5)
102  NEXT K
110  P=26*X(1)**2+77*X(2)+54*X(3)
120  IF P > M THEN 160
130  GO TO 170
160  A(1)=X(1), A(2)=X(2), A(3)=X(3)
165  M=P
170  NEXT I
180  NEXT J
190  PRINT A(1), A(2), A(3), M
200  STOP
210  END
```

And, of course, the technique works on problems where the answer is far from obvious.

A Fifteen-by-Two-Hundred Nonlinear System **12**

Consider the following nonlinear system of 15 equations and 200 variables:

$$X_6^2 \sum_{i=1}^{200} X_i = 25,000$$

$$X_7^2 \sum_{i=1}^{200} X_i = 25,000$$

.
.
.

$$X_{20}^2 \sum_{i=1}^{200} X_i = 25,000$$

where $-32 \leqslant X_i \leqslant 33$ for $i = 1, 2, 3, \ldots, 200$.

We transform this system into the following 200-variable nonlinear minimization problem and solve it using multistage Monte Carlo.

We have minimize

$$f(X_1, X_2, \ldots, X_{200}) = |\, X_6^2 \sum_{i=1}^{200} X_i - 25{,}000 \,|$$
$$+ |\, X_7^2 \sum_{i=1}^{200} X_i - 25{,}000 \,| + \ldots |\, X_{20}^2 \sum_{i=1}^{200} X_i - 25{,}000 \,|$$

subject to $-32 \leqslant X_i \leqslant 33$ for $i = 1, 2, 3, \ldots, 200$.

The 200-dimensional rectangles of ever decreasing size travel across 200-dimensional space (bounded by $-32 \leqslant X_i \leqslant 33$) to a solution. Only 50,000 sample answers had to be looked at. The computer reduced the size of the rectangles (always centered at the best answer so far) 100 times. After each reduction a sample of 500 new answers was looked at in the ever changing and sliding reduced rectangle area. The trail led right to the following solution to the 15×200 nonlinear system (and the answer checks).

The solution is in the pattern:

$$
\begin{array}{ccccc}
X_1 & X_2 & X_3 & X_4 & X_5 \\
X_6 & X_7 & X_8 & X_9 & X_{10} \\
\cdot & \cdot & \cdot & \cdot & \cdot \\
\cdot & \cdot & \cdot & \cdot & \cdot \\
\cdot & \cdot & \cdot & \cdot & \cdot \\
X_{196} & X_{197} & X_{198} & X_{199} & X_{200}
\end{array}
$$

_____EXERCISE

12.1   Write BASIC and FORTRAN programs to solve the preceding problem.

-22.8039963	-22.8039958	-22.8039958	22.8039958	22.8039958
-22.8039958	-22.8039958	22.8039958	22.8039958	22.8039958
-22.8039958	-22.8039958	22.8039958	22.8039958	-22.8039958

-22.8039958	22.8039958	22.8039958	22.8039958	22.8039958
-26.2368251	27.7609651	-.8142509	-15.8959764	24.1127135
2.6918461	-11.8833341	-5.2286857	-28.2683039	13.2945644
-13.9132256	10.1084952	-20.1018035	-12.5388738	5.2144575
-1.2985621	-3.5214195	-31.0246239	4.1825394	9.8263589
-10.5988924	-.0278714	21.7854083	19.8372469	20.4954547
-27.8543992	-4.4173719	-31.7260958	26.1188561	-23.0591218
17.6060265	4.5778259	14.5654408	26.4220716	-26.0062291
25.3786871	17.1689408	11.1989529	-19.3879538	-11.9475866
4.6300621	-3.7612520	-14.6722678	2.4031466	-15.2965858
-20.5278624	6.5583794	4.0605896	19.4323183	-20.8964482
-.7307868	-19.2653909	11.9293682	25.5487804	-24.6064936
-31.6604253	26.3131727	32.9027650	-24.5834311	6.7696832
-17.6032443	-7.9156645	-27.9518762	25.1915525	-19.0668118
25.8128877	-10.8698812	.6313099	2.5107978	9.0057504
-.6605025	21.8803371	29.4197814	-9.8278877	-10.1382632
-24.2623956	3.7913130	-22.1485691	21.6710907	15.2049599
10.4159386	25.6865219	9.9797046	-27.8652507	10.8402782
27.5006825	-5.1067989	26.2604211	-25.4349883	6.6180843
-18.9886850	-3.5445535	-.0393232	-4.4482739	-12.2971538
-9.3056616	-25.5849746	20.9832074	28.4674834	-16.1083041
7.1683979	-8.9829671	-1.0295931	27.6011598	-9.7448871
-12.6603314	.4947381	17.2246479	2.7855267	7.9335555
5.3187983	11.4729504	-5.2225470	29.0808639	11.2141225
16.7630181	-11.7982818	-2.5190495	15.9526234	-24.2033842
-14.5156751	23.8158933	-23.6638128	7.4289941	28.7369306
16.2257355	10.4173294	-11.0450442	30.8932887	-27.2922594
1.9649694	-6.6703278	-31.8826108	16.6883190	-10.6130481
19.1278266	6.3825810	28.6721414	-16.9460743	-18.6020068
-11.9842101	1.8152777	5.9480670	-22.7812571	-3.9206163
.4858832	27.8103009	-2.7848272	22.8953027	28.8358406
.7383760	2.6085942	15.5747907	-31.7858838	6.3015486
-7.1632610	5.5174245	-28.1528520	-15.2969651	-23.5469694
-17.2634786	3.4693522	-2.9667585	-16.8648093	26.5354287
3.8628921	4.5681794	-4.5132315	7.5690316	-.6045224
1.8927580	.2888136	-8.7226708	-16.0346029	1.8322048
2.7928611	14.3079436	-23.1917161	13.5977377	-29.0324168

This solution is accurate to eight decimal places in all 200 variables and 15 equations (seven places were printed for ease of reading). The total error term in all 15 equations combined is 0.00000001. In the solution region ($-32 \leqslant X_i \leqslant 33$ for $i = 1, 2, 3, \ldots, 200$) there were about 1×10^{1960} feasible solutions of about eight decimals. And yet a trail of only 50,000 samples led right to an accurate solution.

Balancing Equations 13

Consider the system of equations

$$\sum_{i=1}^{16} X_i = 1,000$$

$$\sum_{i=1}^{14} X_i X_{i+1} X_{i+2} = 14,000$$

$$\sum_{i=1}^{15} X_i X_{i+1}^2 = 15,000$$

$$\sum_{i=1}^{15} X_i^2 X_{i+1} = 16,000$$

$$\sum_{i=1}^{16} X_i^3 = 12,000$$

subject to $-150 \leqslant X_i \leqslant 250$ for $i = 1, 2, 3, \ldots, 16$.
We translate this problem to minimize

$$f(X_1, X_2, \ldots, X_{16}) = |\sum_{i=1}^{16} X_i - 1,000|$$

$$+ |\sum_{i=1}^{14} X_i X_{i+1} X_{i+2} - 14,000| + |\sum_{i=1}^{15} X_i X_{i+1}^2 - 15,000|$$

$$+ \mid \sum_{i=1}^{15} X_i^2 X_{i+1} - 16,000 \mid + \mid \sum_{i=1}^{16} X_i^3 - 12,000 \mid$$

subject to $- 150 \leqslant X_i \leqslant 250$ for $i = 1, 2, 3, \ldots, 16$ and could then try to solve it using multistage. Let's say that we select a focusing factor of $F = 2$ for all 16 variables. Set the J loop (which controls the number of focuses) to 30. The idea is to randomly sample 1,000 feasible solutions and then divide the 16 bounds by $F = 2^2$. Then sample another 1,000 feasible solutions around the best answer so far and divide the bounds (always centered at the best answer so far) by $F = 2^3$, etc., until the multistage program draws the last (30th in this case) sample of a 1,000 when $F = 2^{30}$.

This may solve the problem. However, it might not because the first equation (without the squared and cubed terms) will produce errors in the multistage focusing process that are smaller in relative magnitude than the ones in the other equations. So the program might solve the second, third, fourth and fifth equations simultaneously, but miss the first one. This can sometimes be prevented by drawing a much larger sample of feasible solutions at each focus stage.

But a more efficient technique would be to weight the error terms in the first equation for, say, the first 25 focuses, and then use the regular transformation on the last five focuses.

We could try to minimize

$$f(X_1, X_2, X_3, \ldots, X_{16}) = \mid \sum_{i=1}^{16} X_i - 1,000 \mid^3$$

$$+ \mid \sum_{i=1}^{14} X_i X_{i+1} X_{i+2} - 14,000 \mid + \mid \sum_{i=1}^{15} X_i X_{i+1}^2 - 15,000 \mid$$

$$+ \mid \sum_{i=1}^{15} X_i^2 X_{i+1} - 16,000 \mid + \mid \sum_{i=1}^{16} X_i^3 - 12,000 \mid$$

subject to $-150 \leqslant X_i \leqslant 250$ for $i = 1, 2, 3, \ldots, 16$ for the first 25 focuses (to get us in the right region) and then switch to minimize

$$f(X_1, X_2, X_3, \ldots, X_{16}) = \left| \sum_{i=1}^{16} X_i - 1,000 \right|$$

$$+ \left| \sum_{i=1}^{14} X_i X_{i+1} X_{i+2} - 14,000 \right| + \left| \sum_{i=1}^{15} X_i X_{i+1}^2 - 15,000 \right|$$

$$+ \left| \sum_{i=1}^{15} X_i^2 X_{i+1} - 16,000 \right| + \left| \sum_{i=1}^{16} X_i^3 - 12,000 \right|$$

subject to $-150 \leqslant X_i \leqslant 250$ for $i = 1, 2, 3, \ldots, 16$ for the last five focuses. We could also try to minimize

$$f(X_1, X_2, X_3, \ldots, X_{16}) = \left| \sum_{i=1}^{16} X_i - 1,000 \right|^2$$

$$+ \left| \sum_{i=1}^{14} X_i X_{i+1} X_{i+2} - 14,000 \right| + \left| \sum_{i=1}^{15} X_i X_{i+1}^2 - 15,000 \right|$$

$$+ \left| \sum_{i=1}^{15} X_i^2 X_{i+1} - 16,000 \right| + \left| \sum_{i=1}^{16} X_i^3 - 12,000 \right|$$

subject to $-150 \leqslant X_i \leqslant 250$ for $i = 1, 2, 3, \ldots, 16$ for 25 focuses and then switch to minimize

$$f(X_1, X_2, X_3, \ldots, X_{16}) = \left| \sum_{i=1}^{16} X_i - 1,000 \right|$$

$$+ \left| \sum_{i=1}^{15} X_i X_{i+1} X_{i+2} - 14,000 \right| + \left| \sum_{i=1}^{15} X_i X_{i+1}^2 - 15,000 \right|$$

$$+ \left| \sum_{i=1}^{15} X_i^2 X_{i+1} - 16,000 \right| + \left| \sum_{i=1}^{16} X_i^3 - 12,000 \right|$$

subject to $-150 \leqslant X_i \leqslant 250$ for $i = 1, 2, 3, \ldots, 16$ for the last five focuses.

The author has had some success with using these "balancing transformations" when solving nonlinear systems of equations where the functional forms of the transformed equation terms are quite different.

An Eleven-Thousand-Variable Nonlinear Problem **14**

The problem here is to write a compact FORTRAN IV program that will produce ten to fifteen solutions (accurate to 14 decimal places in all 11,000 variables) to the equation

$$\sum_{i=1}^{10,998} (X_i + X_{i+2})X_{i+1} = 5,000$$

subject to $-10 \leqslant X_i \leqslant 10$ for $i = 1, 2, 3, \ldots, 11,000$.
The problem is transformed to minimize

$$f(X_1, X_2, X_3, \ldots, X_{11,000})$$

$$= \left| \sum_{i=1}^{10,998} (X_i + X_{i+2})X_{i+1} - 5,000 \right|$$

subject to $-10 \leqslant X_i \leqslant 10$ for $i = 1, 2, 3, \ldots, 11,000$.
The 54-statement multistage FORTRAN IV program drives the function value down to zero (hence solving the equation) by creating 11,000-dimensional rectangles that rocket across the feasible solution space relentlessly pursuing a solution. Because there are 21,997 terms in the problem, each function evaluation could use up several seconds of computer time. Therefore, the program only draws 400 sample answers in total

on its way to a solution. The *DO* loop in lines 5.000 through
52.000 tries to produce 19 solutions, so that if we get a local
optimal or two we will still have plenty of solutions.

Note that we just print the function value of each solution.
Printing each variable value would require hundreds of pages.
However, if the reader wishes to have the variable values printed
along with the function value, just remove line 45.000 (as
indicated).

The program follows:

```
1.000        DOUBLE PRECISION X(11000), A(11000)
2.000        DOUBLE PRECISION P1, P, M, AU, U, L
3.000        INTEGER Z
4.000        INPUT IY
5.000        DO 75 IB=1, 19
6.000        F=3.00
7.000        DO1 I=1, 11000
8.000    1   A(I)=0.0
9.000        M=1.0 E70
10.000       DO 19 J=1, 40
11.000       Z=10
12.000       DO 3 I=1, Z
13.000       DO 4 K=1, 11000
14.000       IF (A(K)-10.0/F**J.LT.-10.0) GO TO 50
15.000       GO TO 60
16.000   50  L=-10.0
17.000       GO TO 65
18.000   60  L=A(K)-10.0F**J
19.000   65  IF (A(K)+10.0/F**J.GT.10.0) GO TO 80
20.000       GO TO 90
21.000   80  AU=10.0-L
22.000       GO TO 100
23.000   90  AU=A(K)+10.0/F**J-L
24.000   100 CALL RANDOM (IY, JY, U)
25.000       X(K)=L+U*AU
```

```
26.000        IY=JY
27.000   4    CONTINUE
28.000        P1=0.0
29.000        DO 666 IT=1, 10998
30.000  666   P1=P1+(X(IT)+X(IT+2))*X(IT+1)
31.000        P=DABS(P1-5000.0)
32.000        IF(P.LT.M) GO TO 200
33.000        GO TO 3
34.000  200   M=P
35.000        DO 11 I1=1, 11000
36.000        A(I1)=X(I1)
37.000   11   CONTINUE
38.000   3    CONTINUE
39.000   19   CONTINUE
40.000        WRITE(108, 302)M
41.000  302   FORMAT (' ', F20.12)
42.000  C     REMOVE THE FOLLOWING STATEMENT
43.000  C     IF YOU WANT THE VARIABLE
44.000  C     VALUES OF THE SOLUTION PRINTED
45.000        GO TO 75
46.000        K1=0
47.000        DO 10 L1=1, 5500
48.000        WRITE(108, 300)A(K1+1), A(K1+2)
49.000  300   FORMAT(' ', 3F20.12)
50.000        K1=K1+2
51.000   10   CONTINUE
52.000   75   CONTINUE
53.000        STOP
54.000        END


6     REM TRANSLATION OF PRECEDING
7     REM FORTRAN PROGRAM INTO BASIC
8     REM TO PRINT SEVEN PLACE
9     REM ACCURACY FOR 1 ANSWER
10    REM YOU NEED A BIT OF COMPUTER
11    REM TIME FOR THIS ONE
```

```
12    DIM X(11000), A(11000)
13    X=1
14    F=3.00
15    M=1.0 E65
16    FOR I2=1 TO 11000
17    A(I2)=0.0
18    NEXT I2
20    FOR J=1 TO 35
22    Z=10
23    FOR I=1 TO Z
24    FOR K=1 TO 11000
30    IF A(K)-10.0/F**J < -10.0 THEN 50
40    GO TO 60
50    L=-10.0
55    GO TO 65
60    L=A(K)-10.0/F**J
65    IF A(K)+10.0/F**J > 10.0 THEN 80
70    GO TO 90
80    U=10.0-L
85    GO TO 100
90    U=A(K)+10.0/F**J-L
100   X(K)=L+RND(X)*U
102   NEXT K
105   P1=0.0
107   FOR IT=1, 10998
110   P1=P1+(X(IT)+X(IT+2))*X(IT+1)
115   P=ABS(P1-5000.0)
120   IF P < M THEN 132
130   GO TO 170
132   FOR I1=1 TO 11000
134   A(I1)=X(I1)
136   NEXT I1
138   M=P
170   NEXT I
180   NEXT J
182   PRINT M
```

```
183  REM REMOVE THE FOLLOWING STATEMENT
184  REM IF YOU WANT THE VARIABLE
185  REM VALUES OF THE SOLUTION PRINTED
186  GO TO 275
188  K1=0
190  FOR L1=1, 5500
192  PRINT A(K1+1), A(K1+2)
194  K1=K1+2
196  NEXT L1
275  STOP
280  END
```

Printout of 16 Solutions from the FORTRAN Program Run

	error term	
.000000000000	solution 1
363.818215588401	local optimal
.000000000043	solution 2
.000000000000	solution 3
.000000000000	solution 4
.000000000000	solution 5
.000000000000	solution 6
.000000000000	solution 7
.000000000000	solution 8
.000000000000	solution 9
.000000000000	solution 10
.000000000000	solution 11
.000000000000	solution 12
.000000000000	solution 13
.000000000000	solution 14
.000000000000	solution 15
764.415592702559	local optimal
.000000000000	solution 16
64.425172236399	local optimal

Notice that the program produced three local optimals and 16 very accurate solutions. Drawing more than 400 sample answers would completely eliminate local optimals from this problem. Each solution used about 30 minutes of computer time on the University of Wisconsin-Green Bay's Xerox Sigma Six computer. The double precision arithmetic added greatly to the time.

The program isn't too difficult to follow. It just creates free-floating ever decreasing (in size) rectangles centered about the best answer so far that rocket across the sampling distribution until they get on the trail of a solution. Then the rectangles close in and find the solution. We were also helped in this problem by the existence of many millions of solutions. But the important point is that with multistage you can always cross the feasible solution sampling distribution and arrive at a very accurate or approximate solution, depending on the difficulty of discovering the trails to the optimal. The number of variables makes very little difference up to 20,000 or so.

An Engineering Design Problem 15

Now let's look at an engineering problem. Noble (see Suggested Reading) presents a plane pin-jointed framework. He has five force vectors that are "pinned" together at a common point. He resolves the force vectors into their x and $-y$ components as

$$-c_1 \cos(e_1) - c_2 \cos(e_2) - \ldots - c_5 \cos(e_5) = f_1$$

$$c_1 \sin(e_1) + c_2 \sin(e_2) + \ldots + c_5 \sin(e_5) = f_2$$

where the e_i's are known. Therefore, Noble has a linear system of equations to solve for the forces (c_i's).

The author would like to present an example where the angles are unknown (at the engineering design stage perhaps) and solve the resulting nonlinear system using multistage.

The pin-jointed system we are considering has six forces: $c_1 = 141.0$, $c_2 = 501.0$, $c_3 = 195.0$, $c_4 = 620.0$, $c_5 = 418.0$ and $c_6 = 217.0$. These six force vectors are to be deployed in the first quadrant of the x,y plane such that the total force in the x direction is 1008.184, and the total force in the y direction is 1220.000. Additionally, this pin-jointed framework will be rigidly rotated 0.50 radians at times during operation of this device. At that point, the x and y forces are to be 299.86575 and 1554.0000, respectively. Therefore, we have the following four by six nonlinear system to solve for the initial angles x_1, x_2, x_3, x_4, x_5 and x_6:

$c_1 \cos(x_1) + c_2 \cos(x_2) + c_3 \cos(x_3) + c_4 \cos(x_4)$
$+ c_5 \cos(x_5) + c_6 \cos(x_6) = 1008.184$

$c_1 \sin(x_1) + c_2 \sin(x_2) + c_3 \sin(x_3) + c_4 \sin(x_4)$
$+ c_5 \sin(x_5) + c_6 \sin(x_6) = 1220.000$

$c_1 \cos(x_1 + 0.5) + c_2 \cos(x_2 + 0.5) + c_3 \cos(x_3 + 0.5)$
$+ c_4 \cos(x_4 + 0.5) + c_5 \cos(x_5 + 0.5) + c_6 \cos(x_6 + 0.5)$
$= 299.86575$

$c_1 \sin(x_1 + 0.5) + c_2 \sin(x_2 + 0.5) + c_3 \sin(x_3 + 0.5)$
$+ c_4 \sin(x_4 + 0.5) + c_5 \sin(x_5 + 0.5) + c_6 \sin(x_6 + 0.5)$
$= 1554.00000$

subject to $0 \leqslant x_i \leqslant \pi/2$ radians and $c_1 = 141.0$, $c_2 = 501.0$, $c_3 = 195.0$, $c_4 = 620.0$, $c_5 = 418.0$ and $c_6 = 217.0$.

Let the left-hand side of equation i be L_i. Then we transform our system into a minimization problem as follows: Minimize

$f(x_1, x_2, \ldots, x_6) = |L_1 - 1008.184| + |L_2 - 1220.000|$
$+ |L_3 - 299.86575| + |L_4 - 1554.00000|$

subject to $0 \leqslant x_i \leqslant \pi/2$ radians and the appropriate c's. The double precision multistage program to solve this problem is presented below. A solution is produced once every minute or two.

```
DOUBLE PRECISION C1,C2,C3,C4,C5,C6,PA3,PB3,PA4,PB4
DOUBLE PRECISION X(7), N(7), L(7), A(7), B(7), AU(7)
DOUBLE PRECISION M,PF,P1,P2,P3,P4,PA1,PB1,BA2,PB2
DOUBLE PRECISION H1, H2, H3, H4
INPUT IY
```

```
      DO 75 IB=1, 3
      M=1.0 E30
C     F IS THE FOCUSING ANSWER
      F=2
      DO 1 I=1, 7
      B(I)=0.0
      A(I)=.77
1     N(I)=1.5707963
      C1=141.0; C2=510.0; C3=195.0
      C4=620.0; C5=418.0; C6=217.0
      Z=200
      DO 19 J=1, 50
      DO 3 I=1, Z
C     THE RECTANGLES
      DO 4 K=1, 7
      IF (A(K)-N(K)/F**J.LT.B(K)) GO TO 50
      GO TO 60
50    L(K)=B(K)
      GO TO 65
60    L(K)=A(K)-N(K)/F**J
65    IF (A(K)+N(K)/F**J.GT.N(K)) GO TO 80
      GO TO 90
80    AU(K)=N(K)-L(K)
      GO TO 100
90    AU(K)=A(K)+N(K)/F**J-L(K)
100   CALL RANDOM(IY, JY, U)
      X(K)=L(K)+U*AU(K)
      IY=JY
4     CONTINUE
      X(7)=.50
C     THE FUNCTION
      PA1=C1*DCOS(X(1))+C2*DCOS(X(2))+C3*DCOS(X(3))
      PB1=C4*DCOS(X(4))+C5*DCOS(X(5))+C6*DCOS(X(6))
      P1=DABS(PA1+PB1-1008.184)
      PA2=C1*DSIN(X(1))+C2*DSIN(X(2))+C3*DSIN(X(3))
      PB2=C4*DSIN(S(4))+C5*DSIN(X(5))+C6*DSIN(X(6))
```

```
      P2=DABS(PA2+PB2-1220.000)
      PA3=C1*DCOS(X(1)+X(7))+C2*DCOS(X(2)+(X(7))+C3*DCOS(X(3)+X(7))
      PB3=C4*DCOS(X(4)+X(7))+C5*DCOS(X(5)+X(7))+C6*DCOS(X(6)+X(7))
      P3=DABS(PA3+PB3-299.86575)
      PA4=C1*DSIN(X(1)+X(7))+C2*DSIN(X(2)+X(7))+C3*DSIN(X(3)+X(7))
      PB4=C4*DSIN(X(4)+X(7))+C5*DSIN(X(5)+X(7))+C6*DSIN(X(6)+X(7))
      P4=DABS(PA4+PB4-1554.000)
      PF=P1+P2+P3+P4
      IF(PF.LT.M) GO TO 200
      GO TO 3
200   CONTINUE
      M=PF
      DO 11 I1=1, 7
      A(I1)=X(I1)
      H1=P1; P2=P2; H3=P3; H4=P4
11    CONTINUE
3     CONTINUE
19    CONTINUE
      WRITE(108,304)A(1), A(2), A(3), A(4)
304   FORMAT ('  ', 4F14.7)
      WRITE(108, 306)A(5), A(6), A(7), M
306   FORMAT ('  ', 4F14.7)
      WRITE(108, 308)H1, H2, H3, H4
308   FORMAT('  ', 4F14.7)
75    CONTINUE
      STOP
      END


2     REM ENGINEERING DESIGN PROBLEM
3     REM TRANSLATED INTO BASIC
4     X=1
5     DIM X(7), N(7), L(7), A(7), B(7), U(7)
6     FOR I8=1 TO 3
8     M=1.0E30
9     REM F IS THE FOCUSING FACTOR
10    F=2
11    FOR I2=1 TO 7
12    B(I2)=0.0, A(I2)=.77, N(I2)=1.5707963
13    NEXT I2
```

```
14   C1=141.0, C2=501.0, C3=195.0
15   C4=620.0, C5=418.0, C6=217.0
16   Z=200
17   FOR J=1, 45
18   FOR I=1 TO Z
20   REM THE RECTANGLES
24   FOR K=1 TO 7
30   IF A(K)-N(K)/F**J < B(K) THEN 50
40   GO TO 60
50   L(K)=B(K)
55   GO TO 65
60   L(K)=A(K)-N(K)/F**J
65   IF A(K)+N(K)/F**J > N(K) THEN 80
70   GO TO 90
80   U(K)=N(K)-L(K)
85   GO TO 100
90   U(K)=A(K)+N(K)/F**J-L(K)
100  X(K)=L(K)+RND(X)*U(K)
102  NEXT K
103  X(7)=.50
104  REM THE FUNCTION
105  P1=C1*COS(X(1))+C2*COS(X(2))+C3*COS(X(3))
106  P2=C4*COS(X(4))+C5*COS(X(5))+C6*COS(X(6))
107  R1=ABS(P1+P2-1008.184)
108  P3=C1*SIN(X(1))+C2*SIN(X(2))+C3*SIN(X(3))
109  P4=C4*SIN(X(4))+C5*SIN(X(5))+C0*SIN(X(6))
110  R2=ABS(P3+P4-1220.000)
111  P5=C1*COS(X(1)+X(7))+C2*COS(X(2)+X(7))+C3*COS(X(3)+X(7))
112  P6=C4*COS(X(4)+X(7))+C5*COS(X(5)+X(7))+C6*COS(X(6)+X(7))
113  R3=ABS(P5+P6-299.86575)
114  P7=C1*SIN(X(1)+X(7))+C2*SIN(X(2)+X(7))+C3*SIN(X(3)+X(7))
115  P8=C4*SIN(X(4)+X(7))+C5*SIN(X(5)+X(7))+C6*SIN(X(6)+X(7))
116  R4=ABS(P7+P8-1554.000)
118  P=R1+R2+R3+R4
120  IF P < M THEN 160
130  GO TO 170
160  A(1)=X(1), A(2)=X(2), A(3)=X(3), A(4)=X(4), A(5)=X(5), A(6)=X(6), A(7)=X(7)
162  M=P
164  H1=R1, H2=R2, H3=R3, H4=R4
170  NEXT I
```

```
180   NEXT J
190   PRINT A(1), A(2), A(3), A(4)
195   PRINT A(5), A(6), A(7), M
196   PRINT "EQUATION ERROR TERMS BELOW"
197   PRINT H1, H2, H3, H4
198   PRINT
199   PRINT
200   PRINT
210   PRINT
220   PRINT
230   NEXT I8
240   STOP
250   END
```

The printout of the run of the FORTRAN program is:

X_1=.8644968	X_2=.0393392	X_3=.0304193	X_4 = 1.5596352
X_5=1.5639339	X_6=.2284584	X_7=.5000000	te =.0002416 solution
e_1=.0002387	e_2=.0000000	e_3=.0000000	e_4=.0000028
X_1=1.5164830	X_2=1.5609546	X_3=.6354119	X_4=.0479685
X_5=1.5639186	X_6=.0681574	X_7=.5000000	te =.0002416 solution
e_1=.0002387	e_2=.0000000	e_3=.0000000	e_4=.0000028
X_1=.0000000	X_2=1.0045243	X_3=.0000000	X_4=1.5707963
X_5=.0000000	X_6=1.5381586	X_7=.5000000	te =106.5773851 local optimal
e_1=21.6784872	e_2=39.6817676	e_3=.0000000	e_4=45.2171304

yielding two solutions and a local optimal in about three minutes of computer time on a Xerox Sigma Six. Note that X_7
is the 0.5 radian rigid rotation in the printout. Also, *te* is the
total error and e_i is the error in the *i*th equation.

   Lines 5, 31, 32 and 33 in the forces problem and lines 4.000,
24.000, 25,000 and 26,000 in the 11,000-variable problem
contain the random number generator. The rest is standard
FORTRAN IV and the programs should run on most computers with some format adjustments.

The multistage theory and approach seems rather unbelievable. However, as long as the trails to the optimals are there, solutions to nonlinear multivariate problems are attainable as never before. Bayesian statistics says that it is possible to "learn" from preliminary sampling. Multistage Monte Carlo uses the Bayesian discovery philosophy to revise and redirect the rectangles continually toward the solution.

Problems at the Chemical Plant 16

The West Branch Newberry Chemical Plant has a problem. They have been trying somewhat unsuccessfully to develop their KXZA5 process that is supposed to yield various amounts of 40 chemicals on each run. The input compounds and how they react is well known except for how they react to changing temperature during the 100-minute production run.

However, over the last year West Branch Newberry has done experiments on the KXZA5 process with the new "variable thermal reaction measuring machine" and succeeded in coming up with a yield model based on varying the temperature throughout the KXZA5 process run. The temperature setting control is calibrated from the middle value of 100° Celsius. Therefore all temperature settings are percentages up and down from 100° Celsius. Let X_i be the percent temperature setting at minute i during the 100-minute reaction. For example, if X_5 = 25.81326 that means a 25.81326 percentage increase from the middle setting of 100°. So the temperature would be set at 125.81326° at the start of the fifth minute of the reaction. If X_{39} = –14.27316, this means a 14.27316 percentage decrease from the middle setting of 100°. So the temperature would be set at 85.72684° at the start of the 39th minute of the reaction.

Dr. O'Malley developed the precise yield equations given below and solved them with multistage.

___DR. O'MALLEY'S REPORT

The 40-equation-by-100 variable yield system along with one solution is given here.

The procedure is to load the problem into the multistage program (FORTRAN IV double precision arithmetic was used in this case), adjusting the feasible solutions bounds and constraints as appropriate. A 100-dimensional rectangle inside the feasible solution space was sampled for 2,000 feasible answers and the best was stored. Then the rectangle was reduced by a factor of two in each dimension and another 2,000 sample answers in this reduced (and ever free floating) region were drawn and the best stored. Then another 2,000 sample answers were drawn from a similarly reduced rectangle (always centered around the best answer so far) and the best stored again. This procedure was repeated 60 times and the ever decreasing and ever free-floating rectangles rocketed to a solution to our 40 × 100 system. A trail of only 120,000 feasible solutions led right to a solution even though there were over 1×10^{1000} feasible solutions in the constrained region. The problem and solution follow: Find a solution (accurate to seven decimal places) to the following 40 × 100 nonlinear system of equations in the reqion $-75 \leqslant X_i \leqslant 75$ for i = 1, 2, 3, . . . , 100.

$$X_{98} \ (X_6 + X_9 + X_{15} + X_{18} + X_{19} + X_{20} + X_{32} + X_{34}$$
$$+ X_{37} + X_{57}) = 14{,}109 \text{ units of chemical} \tag{1}$$
$$X_{96} \ (X_3 + X_7 + X_{20} + X_{32} + X_{47} + X_{51} + X_{52} + X_{55}$$
$$+ X_{64} + X_{83}) = 14{,}107 \text{ units of chemical} \tag{2}$$
$$X_{25} \ (X_4 + X_{25} + X_{31} + X_{46} + X_{48} + X_{53} + X_{58} + X_{64}$$
$$+ X_{80} + X_{93}) = 14{,}036 \text{ units of chemical} \tag{3}$$
$$X_{20} \ (X_{25} + X_{42} + X_{46} + X_{62} + X_{63} + X_{71} + X_{78} + X_{83}$$
$$+ X_{84} + X_{90}) = 14{,}031 \text{ units of chemical} \tag{4}$$
$$X_{64} \ (X_5 + X_{12} + X_{14} + X_{26} + X_{32} + X_{53} + X_{59} + X_{74}$$
$$+ X_{77} + X_{84}) = 14{,}075 \text{ units of chemical} \tag{5}$$
$$X_7 \ (X_{26} + X_{31} + X_{38} + X_{46} + X_{63} + X_{65} + X_{70} + X_{77}$$
$$+ X_{79} + X_{90}) = 14{,}018 \text{ units of chemical} \tag{6}$$
$$X_{71} \ (X_2 + X_{11} + X_{20} + X_{30} + X_{72} + X_{73} + X_{75} + X_{91}$$
$$+ X_{97} + X_{99}) = 14{,}082 \text{ units of chemical} \tag{7}$$
$$X_{50} \ (X_{19} + X_{20} + X_{31} + X_{39} + X_{53} + X_{54} + 2X_{69}$$
$$+ X_{71} + X_{84}) = 14{,}061 \text{ units of chemical} \tag{8}$$
$$X_{29} \ (X_{11} + X_{35} + X_{36} + X_{44} + X_{51} + X_{60} + X_{65} + X_{72}$$
$$+ X_{74} + X_{95}) = 14{,}040 \text{ units of chemical} \tag{9}$$
$$X_{74} \ (X_3 + X_{15} + X_{36} + X_{45} + X_{52} + X_{61} + X_{68} + X_{83}$$
$$+ X_{89} + X_{90}) = 14{,}085 \text{ units of chemical} \tag{10}$$
$$X_{32} \ (X_{26} + X_{29} + 2X_{40} + X_{44} + X_{58} + X_{84} + X_{87}$$
$$+ 2X_{91}) - 14{,}043 \text{ units of chemical} \tag{11}$$
$$X_{22} \ (X_{12} + X_{36} + X_{37} + X_{41} + X_{46} + X_{62} + X_{65}$$
$$+ 2X_{86} + X_{93}) + 14{,}033 \text{ units of chemical} \tag{12}$$
$$X_{76} \ (X_{23} + X_{31} + X_{37} + X_{41} + X_{51} + X_{62} + X_{66} + X_{68}$$
$$+ X_{72} + X_{85}) = 14{,}087 \text{ units of chemical} \tag{13}$$
$$X_{26} \ (X_1 + X_9 + X_{11} + X_{25} + X_{27} + X_{45} + X_{61} + X_{70}$$
$$+ X_{75} + X_{94}) = 14{,}037 \text{ units of chemical} \tag{14}$$
$$X_{68} \ (2X_{11} + X_{15} + X_{22} + X_{24} + X_{35} + 2X_{53} + X_{70}$$
$$+ X_{79}) = 14{,}079 \text{ units of chemical} \tag{15}$$
$$X_{30} \ (X_{10} + X_{16} + X_{29} + X_{33} + X_{40} + X_{59} + X_{69} + X_{73}$$
$$+ X_{79} + X_{86}) = 14{,}041 \text{ units of chemical} \tag{16}$$

X_{99} $(2X_5 + X_8 + X_{16} + X_{20} + X_{33} + X_{36} + X_{43} + X_{63}$
$+ X_{93}$ $) = 14,110$ units of chemical   (17)

X_{80} $(X_{28} + 2X_{50} + X_{51} + X_{52} + X_{55} + X_{56} + 2X_{58}$
$+ X_{85}$ $) = 14,091$ units of chemical   (18)

X_{55} $(X_{10} + X_{11} + X_{15} + X_{45} + X_{58} + X_{63} + X_{75} + X_{82}$
$+ X_{90} + X_{92}$ $) = 14,066$ units of chemical   (19)

X_{40} $(X_8 + X_{14} + X_{33} + X_{55} + X_{62} + X_{67} + X_{73} + X_{77}$
$+ X_{80} + X_{81}$ $) = 14,051$ units of chemical   (20)

X_{53} $(X_3 + X_{14} + X_{31} + X_{34} + X_{40} + X_{47} + X_{56} + X_{60}$
$+ X_{62} + X_{77}) = 14,064$ units of chemical   (21)

X_{41} $(X_2 + X_8 + X_{18} + X_{37} + X_{54} + X_{62} + X_{82} + X_{88}$
$+ X_{95} + X_{97}$ $) + 14,052$ units of chemical   (22)

X_{13} $(2X_8 + X_{29} + X_{39} + X_{42} + X_{43} + X_{48} + X_{58} + X_{85}$
$+ X_{90}) = 14,024$ units of chemical   (23)

X_{16} $(2X_{20} + X_{21} + X_{41} + X_{65} + X_{67} + X_{76} + X_{84} + X_{90}$
$+ X_{98}$ $) = 14,027$ units of chemical   (24)

X_{60} $(X_{10} + X_{18} + X_{26} + 2X_{33} + X_{35} + X_{42} + X_{45} + X_{56}$
$+ X_{69}$ $) = 14,071$ units of chemical   (25)

X_{83} $(X_5 + X_{12} + X_{14} + X_{15} + X_{22} + X_{30} + X_{60} + X_{75}$
$+ X_{85} + X_{94}$ $) = 14,094$ units of chemical   (26)

X_{95} $(X_7 + X_{11} + X_{18} + X_{54} + X_{55} + X_{58} + X_{59} + X_{60}$
$+ X_{73} + X_{90}$ $) = 14,106$ units of chemical   (27)

X_{57} $(X_7 + X_{13} + X_{15} + X_{23} + X_{47} + X_{68} + X_{69} + X_{71}$
$+ X_{75} + X_{84}$ $) = 14,068$ units of chemical   (28)

X_{72} $(X_7 + X_{10} + X_{19} + X_{22} + X_{28} + X_{29} + X_{32} + X_{53}$
$+ X_{81} + X_{93}$ $) = 14,083$ units of chemical   (29)

X_{14} $(X_{11} + X_{18} + X_{19} + X_{25} + X_{45} + X_{67} + 2X_{71} + X_{81}$
$+ X_{82}$ $) = 14,025$ units of chemical   (30)

X_{21} $(X_{12} + X_{24} + X_{28} + X_{54} + X_{55} + X_{58} + X_{77} + X_{79}$
$+ X_{80} + X_{81}$ $) = 14,032$ units of chemical   (31)

X_{59} $(X_4 + X_5 + X_8 + X_{10} + X_{25} + X_{26} + X_{51} + X_{71}$
$+ X_{77} + X_{94}$ $) = 14,070$ units of chemical   (32)

$$X_2(X_3 + X_5 + X_{18} + X_{19} + X_{27} + X_{29} + X_{40} + X_{43}$$
$$+ X_{55} + X_{96}) = 14{,}013 \text{ units of chemical} \tag{33}$$
$$X_{44}(X_3 + X_{20} + 5X_{26} + X_{68} + X_{86} + X_{92})$$
$$= 14{,}055 \text{ units of chemical} \tag{34}$$
$$X_9(X_3 + X_9 + X_{28} + X_{56} + X_{68} + X_{73} + X_{82} + X_{88}$$
$$+ X_{90} + X_{97}) = 14{,}020 \text{ units of chemical} \tag{35}$$
$$X_{92}(2X_4 + X_{36} + X_{37} + X_{49} + X_{52} + X_{61} + X_{71} + X_{74}$$
$$+ X_{98}) = 14{,}103 \text{ units of chemical} \tag{36}$$
$$X_{73}(X_{23} + X_{34} + X_{35} + X_{37} + X_{51} + X_{58} + X_{67} + X_{73}$$
$$+ X_{88} + X_{97}) = 14{,}084 \text{ units of chemical} \tag{37}$$
$$X_{28}(X_6 + X_7 + X_8 + X_{15} + X_{18} + X_{32} + X_{51} + X_{69}$$
$$+ X_{90} + X_{97}) = 14{,}039 \text{ units of chemical} \tag{38}$$
$$X_{46}(X_{11} + X_{23} + X_{26} + X_{37} + X_{38} + X_{48} + X_{49} + X_{54}$$
$$+ X_{65} + X_{98}) = 14{,}057 \text{ units of chemical} \tag{39}$$
$$X_{34}(X_4 + X_5 + X_{17} + X_{18} + 2X_{29} + X_{43} + X_{53} + X_{62}$$
$$+ X_{100}) = 14{,}045 \text{ units of chemical} \tag{40}$$

Let the left-hand side of equation i be L_i ($i = 1, 2, 3, \ldots, 40$). Then we transform our nonlinear system to a minimization problem as follows: Minimize

$$f(X_1, X_2, X_3, \ldots, X_{100}) = |L_1 - 14{,}109| + |L_2 - 14{,}107|$$
$$+ |L_3 - 14{,}036| + |L_4 - 14{,}031| + |L_5 - 14{,}075|$$
$$+ |L_6 - 14{,}018| + |L_7 - 14{,}082| + |L_8 - 14{,}061|$$
$$+ |L_9 - 14{,}040| + |L_{10} - 14{,}085| + |L_{11} - 14{,}043|$$
$$+ |L_{12} - 14{,}033| + |L_{13} - 14{,}087| + |L_{14} - 14{,}037|$$
$$+ |L_{15} - 14{,}079| + |L_{16} - 14{,}041| + |L_{17} - 14{,}110|$$
$$+ |L_{18} - 14{,}091| + |L_{19} - 14{,}066| + |L_{20} - 14{,}051|$$
$$+ |L_{21} - 14{,}064| + |L_{22} - 14{,}052| + |L_{23} - 14{,}024|$$
$$+ |L_{24} - 14{,}027| + |L_{25} - 14{,}071| + |L_{26} - 14{,}094|$$
$$+ |L_{27} - 14{,}106| + |L_{28} - 14{,}068| + |L_{29} - 14{,}083|$$

$+ \mid L_{30} - 14{,}025 \mid + \mid L_{31} - 14{,}032 \mid + \mid L_{32} - 14{,}070 \mid$
$+ \mid L_{33} - 14{,}013 \mid + \mid L_{34} - 14{,}055 \mid + \mid L_{35} - 14{,}020 \mid$
$+ \mid L_{36} - 14{,}103 \mid + \mid L_{37} - 14{,}084 \mid + \mid L_{38} - 14{,}039 \mid$
$+ \mid L_{39} - 14{,}057 \mid + \mid L_{40} - 14{,}045 \mid$

subject to $- 75 \leqslant X_i \leqslant 75$ for $i = 1, 2, 3, \ldots, 100$.

The solution is:

X1=21.0569628	X2=38.7825626	X3=-3.7233783
X4=-30.0590271	X5=64.6863305	X6=36.7312851
X7=44.0493689	X8=39.9081255	X9=42.9448159
X10=7.0442638	X11=-13.3223920	X12=49.7685233
X13=40.7783964	X14=40.3555513	X15=-5.9864884
X16=33.3025065	X17=37.0357122	X18=35.0390916
X19=39.4987305	X20=39.5469232	X21=33.3511273
X22=41.7371302	X23=38.1652144	X24=71.7026254
X25=47.9502716	X26=44.2463747	X27=40.4590801
X28=42.9636033	X29=43.2708305	X30=41.3345264
X31=37.4026916	X32=42.3895859	X33=36.7114294
X34=38.5738887	X35=60.1338703	X36=33.7005915
X37=37.0284081	X38=-13.8881715	X39=54.4190161
X40=33.6066588	X41=41.3654978	X42=39.0596713
X43=16.7143275	X44=37.3323559	X45=33.1477927
X46=49.9270701	X47=66.3673911	X48=39.1401622
X49=42.6184527	X50=33.2031603	X51=9.8934927
X52=49.2622508	X53=36.4405230	X54=32.6751421
X55=54.2268613	X56=48.8395346	X57=34.6443041
X58=37.6624214	X59=42.6342352	X60=36.3557876
X61=54.2342759	X62=54.8854266	X63=38.8037482
X64=31.8062375	X65=33.4404665	X66=-16.4060372
X67=57.3919609	X68=52.4803695	X69=46.1025810
X70=16.1520757	X71=44.9243393	X72=44.4040041
X73=41.1823469	X74=42.3504670	X75=32.8172079

X76=48.1654482 X77=33.2804146 X78=-49.6315784
X79=38.2962639 X80=41.4235393 X81=18.7360090
X82=39.2456864 X83=41.9306038 X84=46.3712573
X85=-6.7480013 X86=17.5406915 X87=30.3463415
X88=-16.1054135 X89=36.9630012 X90=40.5729104
X91=12.4206500 X92=49.4065914 X93=1.0260374
X94=41.8062398 X95=40.1793603 X96=37.5436458
X97=38.0650044 X98=41.4470122 X99=38.2295362
X100=36.4867122

Remember that the answer checks when substituted back into the equations.

The error term in each equation is:

.000000000015 equation 1
.000000000065 equation 2
.000000000015   ”
.000000000007   ”
.000000000051   ”
.000000000005   ”
.000000000002   ”
.000000000025   ”
.000000000044   ”
.000000000015   ”
.000019841264   ”
.000000000012   ”
.000000000013   ”
.000000000002   ”
.000000000011   ”
.000000000025   ”
.000000000005   ”
.000000000006   ”
.000000000001   ”
.000000000009   ”

.000000000012   ,,
.000000000021   ,,
.000000000017   ,,
.000000000032   ,,
.000000000059   ,,
.000000000011   ,,
.000000000016   ,,
.000000141260   ,,
.000000000003   ,,
.000000000000   ,,
.000000000011   ,,
.000000000019   ,,
.000000000009   ,,
.000000000040   ,,
.000062489366   ,,
.000000000025   ,,
.000000000006   ,,
.000000000061   ,,
.000000005478   ,,
.000000000002 equation 40

Respectfully submitted,

Dr. K.O. O'Malley

So the company has a solution to this very profitable process. However, West Branch Newberry wants several alternative solutions to choose from and they want a standard program to record and change as yields may change. In addition, Dr. O'Malley recently took a job with another firm and no one can find his program tape.

Therefore, write a new BASIC program and a new FOR-TRAN program based on Dr. O'Malley's report description to repeatedly solve West Branch Newberry's yield system. The computer run will require a lot of time.

Exercises to Part II

1. Study the market research chapter in Part I carefully and then help the Eagle Rock Portland Corporation do their following quality control study. Eagle Rock Portland manufacturers six products, A, B, C, D, E and F. They are extremely proud of the quality of their products and do much quality control to protect their reputation and corporate good name. It costs \$7, \$3, \$8, \$6, \$1 and \$4.50 to test one unit of A, B, C, D, E and F, respectively. They want to draw the minimum cost number of samples so that they will be at least 95% sure of estimating the proportion of defectives of A, B, C, D, E and F to within 0.015, 0.025, 0.01, 0.02, 0.01 and 0.012, respectively. This 95% certainty is per individual product. Overall they require 85% certainty that all six are within their error bounds. Write a BASIC program to solve the problem for Eagle Rock.

2. Write a BASIC program to solve

$$X_1 + 2X_2 + X_3 = 36$$
$$X_1 + X_2 + X_3 = 27$$
$$X_1 X_2 + X_2 X_3 = 162$$

subject to $0 \leqslant X_i \leqslant 100$ for $i = 1, 2, 3$.

3. Find the (X_1, X_2, X_3) point that minimizes the distance between $6X_1 - 3X_2 + X_3^2 = 18$ and $9X_1 + X_2 + X_3 = 800$.

4. Take a uniform distribution $f(X) = 1/101$ for $X = 0, 1, 2, \ldots, 100$ and draw one million samples of size $M = 40$ (samples taken at random using the random number generator) and calculate $Z = (\bar{X} - U)/(S/\sqrt{M})$ where $U = 50$. Have an array keep track of the frequency of the occurence of the Z values between ±3. Have the printout of this

BASIC program checked against the standard normal curve. This should provide substantial evidence that $Z = (\overline{X} - U)/(S/\sqrt{M})$ is standard normally distributed for any underlying distribution if $M > 30$.

5. Find the seven solutions to $X^7 + 2X^6 + 9X^5 + X^4 + 3X^3 - 19X^2 + 8X + 18 = 0$. (Hint: use complex arithmetic. Build it into your BASIC program.)

6. The Michigan Bluff Electronics Company will build several thousand electrical resistance networks consisting of three resistors in parallel connected in series to two other resistors in parallel. All five resistors have switches that can connect or disconnect the resistors independently. If the resistors are arranged in the pattern

        1   2   3   in parallel
           series connected
           4   5   in parallel

solve for the five resistor values (in ohms) that will meet all of the following switch-throwing combinations:

Switches on	Total ohms required
1, 2, 3, 4, 5	32.727248
1, 4, 5	37.272702
2, 4, 5	47.272702
3, 4, 5	57.272702
1, 2, 4	66.666667
1, 2, 5	56.666667
2, 3, 4	72.000005
2, 3, 5	62.000005

Using the laws for connecting resistors in series and parallel gives us the following system of equations:

$$\cfrac{1}{\cfrac{1}{X_1}+\cfrac{1}{X_2}+\cfrac{1}{X_3}} + \cfrac{1}{\cfrac{1}{X_4}+\cfrac{1}{X_5}} = 32.727248$$

$$\cfrac{1}{X_1} + \cfrac{1}{\cfrac{1}{X_4}+\cfrac{1}{X_5}} = 37.272702$$

$$\cfrac{1}{X_2} + \cfrac{1}{\cfrac{1}{X_4}+\cfrac{1}{X_5}} = 47.272702$$

$$\cfrac{1}{X_3} + \cfrac{1}{\cfrac{1}{X_4}+\cfrac{1}{X_5}} = 57.272702$$

$$\cfrac{1}{\cfrac{1}{X_1}+\cfrac{1}{X_2}} + \cfrac{1}{\cfrac{1}{X_4}} = 66.666667$$

$$\cfrac{1}{\cfrac{1}{X_1}+\cfrac{1}{X_2}} + \cfrac{1}{\cfrac{1}{X_5}} = 56.666667$$

$$\cfrac{1}{\cfrac{1}{X_2}+\cfrac{1}{X_3}} + \cfrac{1}{\cfrac{1}{X_4}} = 72.000005$$

$$\cfrac{1}{\cfrac{1}{X_2}+\cfrac{1}{X_3}} + \cfrac{1}{\cfrac{1}{X_5}} = 62.000005$$

Each resistor must have between 1 and 500 ohms.

7. Write a BASIC program using your standard normal random number generator to approximate the upper 0.05, 0.025, 0.01 and 0.005 t points for 14 degrees of freedom by using a sample scheme similar to the one in exercise 4.

8. Solve the following nonlinear blending problem for the Georgia Key Company at their Tamaraque Blending plant. The X_i's represent input amounts and the right-hand sides of the equations represent output units of their three products:

$$X_1 + X_2 + X_3 + X_4 + X_5 + X_6 + X_7 = 800 \text{ units}$$

$$X_1 X_2 \cdot 5 + X_3 X_4 \cdot 5 + X_5^2 + X_6 + 4X_7 = 16,000 \text{ units}$$

$$2X_i + 9X_2 + 17X_3 + 85X_4 + 19X_5 + 20X_6 + 3X_7$$
$$= 3900 \text{ units}$$

9. The binomial probability distribution is defined as (M/X) $P^X (1-P)^{M-X}$ where M is the number of independent trials, P is the probability of a success and

$$\left(\frac{M}{X}\right) = \frac{M!}{(M-X)! \ X!}$$

Create a binomial table for all possible outcomes for M = 2, 3, 4, 5, . . . , 30 trials and P = 0.01, 0.02, 0.03, 0.04, . . . , 50. This is used in reliability theory.

10. Wakefield Cascade has figured its price quantity curve for product KAX5 for the next year to be either P_1 = $-0.00018X_1$ + 50 or P_1 = $-0.0002X_1$ + 40 or P_1 = $-0.0003X_1$ + 60, depending on the business climate. (P_1 is the price and X_1 is the corresponding demand for KAX5 that this price sets off.) Its costs for manufacturing a unit of KAX5 will be either \$6.50, \$7 or \$8, depending on the outcome of labor negotiations. Write a BASIC program to

find the mini-max solution to maximize profit. (Find the solution so that the minimum profit will be a maximum regardless of which of the nine business circumstances arise.)

11. Translate the BASIC programs that solve the previous ten exercises into FORTRAN.

12. The Poplar Mountain Company has the data below from their Westphalia plant. Find the least squares best straight line (really a plane in this three-variable case) for this data by solving the following least squares normal equations for three variables. We want to fit the model $Y = B_0 + B_1 X_1 + B_2 X_2$ by solving

$$MB_0 + B_1 \ \Sigma X_1 + B_2 \ \Sigma X_2 = \Sigma Y$$

$$B_0 \ \Sigma X_1 + B_1 \ \Sigma X_1^2 + B_2 \ \Sigma X_1 X_2 = \Sigma X_1 Y$$

$$B_0 \ \Sigma X_2 + B_1 \ \Sigma X_1 X_2 + B_2 \ \Sigma X_2^2 = \Sigma X_2 Y$$

for this data

Hourly pay ($) X_1	*Number of breaks per day* X_2	*Number of manufacturing defects* Y
7.00	4	8
9.00	5	6
4.50	4	16
3.90	2	25
8.00	1	10

Poplar Mountain is trying to get a line on the idea that high pay and lots of breaks in work routine lead to less defective products.

Selected Answers

CHAPTER 1

1.1.

```
5   REM CHAPTER 1
10  REM EXERCISE 1.1
15  S=0
20  FOR I=1 TO 1000 STEP 2
25  S=S+I
30  NEXT I
35  PRINT S
40  STOP
45  END
>RUN
17:58    DEC 18   ONE...
 250000
```

1.4.

```
5   REM CHAPTER 1
10  REM EXERCISE 1.4
15  S=0
20  FOR I=10 TO 100
25  S=S+I
```

```
30 NEXT I
35 PRINT S
40 STOP
45 END
>RUN
17:58    DEC 18   TWO...
 5005
```

1.6.

```
 5  REM CHAPTER 1
10 REM EXERCISE 1.6
15 PRINT "FRANCS","DOLLARS"
20 FOR F=1 TO 500
25 D=F/7.
30 PRINTUSING 32,F,D
32: ###.        ####.##
35 NEXT F
40 STOP
45 END
>RUN
17:59   DEC 18   THREE...
FRANCS           DOLLARS
     1.            0.14
     2.            0.29
     3.            0.43
     4.            0.57
     5.            0.71
     6.            0.86
     7.            1.00
     8.            1.14
     9.            1.29
    10.            1.43
    11.            1.57
    12.            1.71
    13.            1.86
    14.            2.00
    15.            2.14
```

16.	2.29
17.	2.43
18.	2.57
19.	2.71
20.	2.86
21.	3.00
22.	3.14
23.	3.29
24.	3.43
25.	3.57
26.	3.71
27.	3.86
28.	4.00
29.	4.14
30.	4.29
31.	4.43
32.	4.57
33.	4.71
34.	4.86
35.	5.00
36.	5.14
37.	5.29
38.	5.43
39.	5.57
40.	5.71
41.	5.86
42.	6.00
43.	6.14
44.	6.29
45.	6.43
46.	6.57
47.	6.71
48.	6.86
49.	7.00
50.	7.14
51.	7.29
52.	7.43
53.	7.57
54.	7.71

55.	7.86
56.	8.00
57.	8.14
58.	8.29
59.	8.43
60.	8.57
61.	8.71
62.	8.86
63.	9.00
64.	9.14
65.	9.29
66.	9.43
67.	9.57
68.	9.71
69.	9.86
70.	10.00
71.	10.14
72.	10.29
73.	10.43
74.	10.57
75.	10.71
76.	10.86
77.	11.00
78.	11.14
79.	11.29
80.	11.43
81.	11.57
82.	11.71
83.	11.86
84.	12.00
85.	12.14
86.	12.29
87.	12.43
88.	12.57
89.	12.71
90.	12.86
91.	13.00
92.	13.14

93.	13.29
94.	13.43
95.	13.57
96.	13.71
97.	13.86
98.	14.00
99.	14.14
100.	14.29
101.	14.43
102.	14.57
103.	14.71
104.	14.86
105.	15.00
106.	15.14
107.	15.29
108.	15.43
109.	15.57
110.	15.71
111.	15.86
112.	16.00
113.	16.14
114.	16.29
115.	16.43
116.	16.57
117.	16.71
118.	16.86
119.	17.00
120.	17.14
121.	17.29
122.	17.43
123.	17.57
124.	17.71
125.	17.86
126.	18.00
127.	18.14
128.	18.29
129.	18.43
130.	18.57

131.	18.71
132.	18.86
133.	19.00
134.	19.14
135.	19.29
136.	19.43
137.	19.57
138.	19.71
139.	19.86
140.	20.00
141.	20.14
142.	20.29
143.	20.43
144.	20.57
145.	20.71
146.	20.86
147.	21.00
148.	21.14
149.	21.29
150.	21.43
151.	21.57
152.	21.71
153.	21.86
154.	22.00
155.	22.14
156.	22.29
157.	22.43
158.	22.57
159.	22.71
160.	22.86
161.	23.00
162.	23.14
163.	23.29
164.	23.43
165.	23.57
166.	23.71
167.	23.86
168.	24.00

169.	24.14
170.	24.29
171.	24.43
172.	24.57
173.	24.71
174.	24.86
175.	25.00
176.	25.14
177.	25.29
178.	25.43
179.	25.57
180.	25.71
181.	25.86
182.	26.00
183.	26.14
184.	26.29
185.	26.43
186.	26.57
187.	26.71
188.	26.86
189.	27.00
190.	27.14
191.	27.29
192.	27.43
193.	27.57
194.	27.71
195.	27.86
196.	28.00
197.	28.14
198.	28.29
199.	28.43
200.	28.57
201.	28.71
202.	28.86
203.	29.00
204.	29.14
205.	29.29
206.	29.43

207.	29.57
208.	29.71
209.	29.86
210.	30.00
211.	30.14
212.	30.29
213.	30.43
214.	30.57
215.	30.71
216.	30.86
217.	31.00
218.	31.14
219.	31.29
220.	31.43
221.	31.57
222.	31.71
223.	31.86
224.	32.00
225.	32.14
226.	32.29
227.	32.43
228.	32.57
229.	32.71
230.	32.86
231.	33.00
232.	33.14
233.	33.29
234.	33.43
235.	33.57
236.	33.71
237.	33.86
238.	34.00
239.	34.14
240.	34.29
241.	34.43
242.	34.57
243.	34.71
244.	34.86
245.	35.00

246.	35.14
247.	35.29
248.	35.43
249.	35.57
250.	35.71
251.	35.86
252.	36.00
253.	36.14
254.	36.29
255.	36.43
256.	36.57
257.	36.71
258.	36.86
259.	37.00
260.	37.14
261.	37.29
262.	37.43
263.	37.57
264.	37.71
265.	37.86
266.	38.00
267.	38.14
268.	38.29
269.	38.43
270.	38.57
271.	38.71
272.	38.86
273.	39.00
274.	39.14
275.	39.29
276.	39.43
277.	39.57
278.	39.71
279.	39.86
280.	40.00
281.	40.14
282.	40.29
283.	40.43

```
284.        40.57
285.        40.71
286.        40.86
287.        41.00
288.        41.14
289.        41.29
290.        41.43
291.        41.57
292.        41.71
293.        41.86
294.        42.00
295.        42.14
296.        42.29
297.        42.43
298.        42.57
299.        42.71
300.        42.86
301.        43.00
302.        43.14
303.        43.29
304.        43.43
305.        43.57
306.        43.71
307.        43.86
308.        44.00
309.        44.14
310.        44.29
311.        44.43
312.        44.57
313.        44.71
314.        44.86
315.        45.00
316.        45.14
317.        45.29
318.        45.43
319.        45.57
320.        45.71
321.        45.86
322.        46.00
```

323.	46.14
324.	46.29
325.	46.43
326.	46.57
327.	46.71
328.	46.86
329.	47.00
330.	47.14
331.	47.29
332.	47.43
333.	47.57
334.	47.71
335.	47.86
336.	48.00
337.	48.14
338.	48.29
339.	48.43
340.	48.57
341.	48.71
342.	48.86
343.	49.00
344.	49.14
345.	49.29
346.	49.43
347.	49.57
348.	49.71
349.	49.86
350.	50.00
351.	50.14
352.	50.29
353.	50.43
354.	50.57
355.	50.71
356.	50.86
357.	51.00
358.	51.14
359.	51.29
360.	51.43
361.	51.57

362.	51.71
363.	51.86
364.	52.00
365.	52.14
366.	52.29
367.	52.43
368.	52.57
369.	52.71
370.	52.86
371.	53.00
372.	53.14
373.	53.29
374.	53.43
375.	53.57
376.	53.71
377.	53.86
378.	54.00
379.	54.14
380.	54.29
381.	54.43
382.	54.57
383.	54.71
384.	54.86
385.	55.00
386.	55.14
387.	55.29
388.	55.43
389.	55.57
390.	55.71
391.	55.86
392.	56.00
393.	56.14
394.	56.29
395.	56.43
396.	56.57
397.	56.71
398.	56.86
399.	57.00
400.	57.14

401.	57.29
402.	57.43
403.	57.57
404.	57.71
405.	57.86
406.	58.00
407.	58.14
408.	58.29
409.	58.43
410.	58.57
411.	58.71
412.	58.86
413.	59.00
414.	59.14
415.	59.29
416.	59.43
417.	59.57
418.	59.71
419.	59.86
420.	60.00
421.	60.14
422.	60.29
423.	60.43
424.	60.57
425.	60.71
426.	60.86
427.	61.00
428.	61.14
429.	61.29
430.	61.43
431.	61.57
432.	61.71
433.	61.86
434.	62.00
435.	62.14
436.	62.29
437.	62.43
438.	62.57
439.	62.71

```
440.        62.86
441.        63.00
442.        63.14
443.        63.29
444.        63.43
445.        63.57
446.        63.71
447.        63.86
448.        64.00
449.        64.14
450.        64.29
451.        64.43
452.        64.57
453.        64.71
454.        64.86
455.        65.00
456.        65.14
457.        65.29
458.        65.43
459.        65.57
460.        65.71
461.        65.86
462.        66.00
463.        66.14
464.        66.29
465.        66.43
466.        66.57
467.        66.71
468.        66.86
469.        67.00
470.        67.14
471.        67.29
472.        67.43
473.        67.57
474.        67.71
475.        67.86
476.        68.00
477.        68.14
478.        68.29
```

479.   68.43
480.   68.57
481.   68.71
482.   68.86
483.   69.00
484.   69.14
485.   69.29
486.   69.43
487.   69.57
488.   69.71
489.   69.86
490.   70.00
491.   70.14
492.   70.29
493.   70.43
494.   70.57
495.   70.71
496.   70.86
497.   71.00
498.   71.14
499.   71.29
500.   71.43

1.8.

```
5  REM CHAPTER 1
10 REM EXERCISE 1.8
11 S=0
12 FOR I=0 TO 29.99 STEP .01
15 X=I+.005
20 S=S+.01*X**3
25 NEXT I
40 PRINT S
45 STOP
50 END
>RUN
18:05   DEC 18   FOUR...
 202500.
```

_____CHAPTER 3

3.1.

```
5   REM CHAPTER 3
10 REM EXERCISE 3.1
15 REM FROM CHART
20 REM N=385
>RUN
18:05    DEC 18  FIVE...
```

3.2.

```
5   REM CHAPTER 3
10 REM EXERCISE 3.2
15 REM FROM CHART
20 REM N=166
>RUN
18:06    DEC 18  SIX...
```

3.3.

```
>5   REM CHAPTER 3
>10 REM EXERCISE 3.3
>15 REM FROM CHART
>20 REM N=4887
```

_____CHAPTER 4

4.2.

```
5   REM CHAPTER 4
10 REM EXERCISE 4.2
15 REM YES
>RUN
18:07    DEC 18  EIGHT...
```

4.3.

```
 5  REM CHAPTER 4
10 REM EXERCISE 4.3
15 REM FROM CHART
20 REM N=9604
>RUN
18:07   DEC 18   NINE...
```

4.4.

```
 5  REM CHAPTER 4
10 REM EXERCISE 4.4
15 REM FROM CHART
20 REM N=1692
>RUN
18:07   DEC 18   TEN...
```

4.5.

```
 5 REM CHAPTER 4
10 REM EXERCISE 4.5
15 REM FROM CHART
20 REM N=1842
>RUN
18:08   DEC 18   ELEVEN..
```

_____PART ONE EXERCISES

1.

```
 5    REM PART 1
10    REM AFTER CHAPTER 7
15    REM EXERCISE 1
20    DIM S(100)
30    FOR K6=1 TO 100
40    READ S(K6)
50    NEXT K6
```

```
 60   N5=100
 70   FOR K1=1 TO 99
 80   B=-999999
 82  FOR M2=1 TO N5
 84   IF S(M2) > B THEN 88
 86   GO TO  95
 88   B=S(M2)
 90  A2=M2
 95  NEXT M2
100  T1=S(N5)
110  S(N5)=B
112  S(A2)=T1
130  N5=N5-1
140  NEXT K1
150  FOR   T5=1 TO 100
160  PRINT T5,S(T5)
170  NEXT T5
180  DATA 242,542,503,493,138
190  DATA 371,831,708,221,259
200  DATA 752,819,821,75,305
210  DATA 788,797,450,169,772
220  DATA 738,298,509,314,852
230  DATA 215,576,78,285,395
240  DATA 143,771,886,413,412
250  DATA 428,52,604,752,552
260  DATA 263,49,32,813,666
270  DATA 362,645,707,95,852
280  DATA 630,699,499,47,900
290  DATA 374,64,250,38,340
300  DATA 777,518,169,188,836
310  DATA 852,807,106,95,952
320  DATA 862,845,55,89,355
330  DATA 628,706,12,97,106
340  DATA 285,323,977,195,333
350  DATA 542,318,947,856,550
360  DATA 420,325,921,830,230
370  DATA 857,528,812,214,445
380  STOP
390  END
```

```
>RUN
18:09    DEC 18   TWELVE...
  1            12
  2            32
  3            38
  4            47
  5            49
  6            52
  7            55
  8            64
  9            75
 10            78
 11            89
 12            95
 13            95
 14            97
 15           106
 16           106
 17           138
 18           143
 19           169
 20           169
 21           188
 22           195
 23           214
 24           215
 25           221
 26           230
 27           242
 28           250
 29           259
 30           263
 31           285
 32           285
 33           298
 34           305
 35           314
 36           318
```

37	323
38	325
39	333
40	340
41	355
42	362
43	371
44	374
45	395
46	412
47	413
48	420
49	428
50	445
51	450
52	493
53	499
54	503
55	509
56	518
57	528
58	542
59	542
60	550
61	552
62	576
63	604
64	628
65	630
66	645
67	666
68	699
69	706
70	707
71	708
72	738
73	752
74	752
75	771
76	772

77	777
78	788
79	797
80	807
81	812
82	813
83	819
84	821
85	830
86	831
87	836
88	845
89	852
90	852
91	852
92	856
93	857
94	862
95	886
96	900
97	921
98	947
99	952
100	977

4.

```
5   REM PART 1
10  REM AFTER CHAPTER 7
15  REM EXERCISE 4
20  B=.02
30  Z=1.96
40  N=INT((Z/(2*B))**2+1)
50  PRINT N
60  STOP
70  END
>RUN
18:12    DEC 18   THIRTEEN...
 2401
```

5.

```
5   REM PART 1
10  REM AFTER CHAPTER 7
15  REM EXERCISE 5
20  B=.09
30  Z=2.33
35  S=.3
40  N=INT(((Z*S)/B)**2+1)
50  PRINT N
60  STOP
70  END
>RUN
18:13    DEC 18  FOURTEEN...
61
```

6.

```
5   REM PART 1
10  REM AFTER CHAPTER 7
15  REM EXERCISE 6
16  S1=0
17  S2=0
18  S3=0
19  S4=0
20  N=4
30  FOR I=1 TO 4
35  READ X,Y
38  S1=S1+X
40  S2=S2+Y
42  S3=S3+X**2
46  S4=S4+X*Y
47  NEXT I
49  B1=(N*S4-S1*S2)/(N*S3-S1**2)
50  M1=S1/4
52  M2=S2/4
55  B0=M2-B1*M1
60  PRINT "SLOPE IS",B1
70  PRINT "Y INTERCEPT IS ",B0
72  DATA 1,2
```

```
74 DATA 1,3
76 DATA 2,4
78 DATA 2,3
79 T1=0
80 S=0
82 FOR J=1 TO 4
84 READ X,Y
86 S=S+(Y-M2)**2
87 T1=T1+(X-M1)**2
88 NEXT J
89 S=S-(B1/4)*(N*S4-S1*S2)
90 S=SQR(S/2)
91 T1=SQR(T1)
92 T=B1/(S/T1)
93 DATA 1,2
94 DATA 1,3
95 DATA 2,4
96 DATA 2,3
97 PRINT "T FORMULA VALUE IS",T
98 PRINT "T CRITICAL VALUES ARE",-2.92,2.92
100 STOP
105 END
>RUN
13:27   DEC 19  RUNDCAA...
SLOPE IS       1
Y INTERCEPT IS            1.50000
T FORMULA VALUE IS        1.41421
T CRITICAL VALUES ARE    -2.92000      2.92000
```

7.

```
5    REM PART 1
10   REM AFTER CHAPTER 7
15   REM EXERCISE 7
17   S1=0
18   S2=0
20   FOR I=1 TO 6
25   READ X
27   S1=S1+X
```

```
30   NEXT I
40   M=S1/6
45   FOR J=1 TO 6
50   READ X
55   S2=S2+(X-M)**2
60   NEXT J
65   S2=SQR(S2/5)
70   DATA 18,19,31,12,17,35
80   DATA 18,19,31,12,17,35
90   PRINT "T FORMULA VALUE IS",T
100  PRINT "T CRITICAL VALUES ARE"
110  PRINT -2.571,2.571
120  PRINT "SO DONT REJECT HO"
130  STOP
140  END
>RUN
13:37    DEC 19   RUNDCAA...
T FORMULA VALUE IS              1.41421
T CRITICAL VALUES ARE
-2.57100          2.57100
SO DONT REJECT HO
```

9.

```
5   REM PART 1
10  REM AFTER CHAPTER 7
15  REM EXERCISE 9
20  M1=1000
25  M2=1000
30  P1=10/1000
35  P2=30/1000
40  P=(10+30)/(1000+1000)
50  Z=(P1-P2)/SQR(P*(1-P)/M1+P*(1-P)/M2
60  PRINT "Z FORMULA VALUE IS",Z
70  PRINT "Z CRITICAL VALUES ARE"
80  PRINT -1.96,1.96
90  PRINT "SO REJECT HO"
95  PRINT "THERE IS A DIFFERENCE"
```

```
100 STOP
105 END
>RUN
13:44    DEC 19   RUNDCAA...
Z FORMULA VALUE IS            -3.19438
Z CRITICAL VALUES ARE.
-1.96000       1.96000
SO REJECT HO
THERE IS A DIFFERENCE
```

12.

```
5  REM PART 1
10 REM AFTER CHAPTER 7
15 REM EXERCISE 12
20 M1=20
30 X1=103
40 S1=5
50 M2=20
60 X2=114
70 S2=4
72 Z=(X1-X2)/SQR(S1**2/20+S2**2/20)
74 PRINT "Z FORMULA VALUE IS",Z
76 PRINT "Z CRITICAL VALUES ARE"
78 PRINT -1.96,1.96
80 PRINT "SO REJECT HO"
90 PRINT "THERE IS A DIFFERENCE"
95 STOP
98 END
100 STOP
105 END
>RUN
13:57    DEC 19   RUNDCAA...
Z FORMULA VALUE IS            -7.68273
Z CRITICAL VALUES ARE
-1.96000       1.96000
SO REJECT HO
THERE IS A DIFFERENCE
```

13.

```
 5  REM PART 1
10  REM AFTER CHAPTER 7
15  REM EXERCISE 13
16  S1=0
17  S2=0
18  S3=0
19  S4=0
20  N=3
30  FOR I=1 TO 3
35  READ X,Y
38  S1=S1+X
40  S2=S2+Y
42  S3=S3+X**2
46  S4=S4+X*Y
47  NEXT I
48  B1=(N*S4-S1*S2)/(N*S3-S1**2)
50  M1=S1/3
52  M2=S2/3
55  B0=M2-B1*M1
60  PRINT "SLOPE IS",B1
70  PRINT "Y INTERCEPT IS",B0
80  DATA 1,1
85  DATA 3,2
90  DATA 2,6
92  STOP
96  END
>RUN
14:03    DEC 19   RUNDCAA...
SLOPE IS          .500000
Y INTERCEPT IS                      2
```

15.

```
 5  REM PART 1
10  REM AFTER CHAPTER 7
15  REM EXERCISE 15
20  P1=63/1000
30  P=.03
```

```
40 Z=(P1-P)/SQR(P*(1-P)/1000)
50 PRINT "Z FORMULA VALUE IS",Z
60 PRINT "Z CRITICAL VALUE IS",1.645
70 PRINT "SO REJECT HO"
80 PRINT "DEFECTIVE RATE IS TOO HIGH"
90 STOP
95 END
>RUN
14:08    DEC 19   RUNDCAA...
Z FORMULA VALUE IS            6.11741
Z CRITICAL VALUE IS          1.64500
SO REJECT HO
DEFECTIVE RATE IS TOO HIGH
```

16.

```
5   REM PART 1
10  REM AFTER CHAPTER 7
15  REM EXERCISE 16
20  P=.25
30  M1=20
32  M2=30
35  M3=10
40  M4=40
45  E1=100*P
50  E2=100*P
55  E3=100*P
60  E4=100*P
62  C1=(M1-E1)**2/E1
64  C2=(M2-E2)**2/E2
66  C3=(M3-E3)**2/E3
68  C4=(M4-E4)**2/E4
70  C=C1+C2+C3+C4
72  PRINT "CHI SQUARE FORMIULA IS",C
74  PRINT"CHI SQUARE CRITICAL VALUE IS",7.81473
76  PRINT "THEY ARE NOT EQUAL"
78  STOP
80  END
>RUN
```

```
14:22    DEC 19   RUNDCAA...
CHI SQUARE FORMIULA IS          20
CHI SQUARE CRITICAL VALUE IS              7.81473
THEY ARE NOT EQUAL
```

20(a).

```
5   REM PART 1
10 REM AFTER CHAPTER 7
15 REM EXERCISE 20
16 REM LEAST SQUARES STRAIGHT LINE
18 S1=0
19 S2=0
20 S3=0
21 S4=0
25 N=7
26 FOR I=1 TO 7
30 READ X,Y
38 S1=S1+X
40 S2=S2+Y
42 S3=S3+X**2
46 S4=S4+X*Y
47 NEXT I
48 B1=(N*S4-S1*S2)/(N*S3-S1**2)
50 M1=S1/7
52 M2=S2/7
55 B0=M2-B1*M1
60 PRINT "SLOPE IS",B1
70 PRINT "Y INTERCEPT IS",B0
80 DATA 5,10
82 DATA 8,12
84 DATA 9,14
86 DATA 10,16
88 DATA 12,17
90 DATA 14,18
92 DATA 16,21
94 STOP
96 END
```

```
>RUN
14:30    DEC 19   RUNDCAA...
SLOPE IS         .882935
Y INTERCEPT IS                    5.03754
```

20(b).

```
1    REM PART 1
2    REM AFTER CHAPTER 7
3    REM EXERCISE 20
4    REM LEAST ABSOLUTE DEVIATION
5    REM STRAIGHT LINE (THREE RUNS)
6    DIM A(2),B(2),L(2),N(2),U(2),X(2)
7    F=2
10   X=1
12   M=9999999
14   FOR I2=1 TO 2
16   A(I2)=0,B(I2)=-20,N(I2)=20
18   NEXT I2
20   FOR J=1 TO 20
21   FOR I=1 TO 700
24   FOR K=1 TO 2
30   IF A(K)-N(K)/F**J < B(K) THEN 50
40   GO TO 60
50   L(K)=B(K)
55   GO TO 65
60   L(K)=A(K)-N(K)/F**J
65   IF A(K)+N(K)/F**J > N(K) THEN 80
70   GO TO 90
80   U(K)=N(K)-L(K)
85   GO TO 100
90 U(K)=A(K)+N(K)/F**J-L(K)
100 X(K)=L(K)+RND(X)*U(K)
102 NEXT K
103 C1=ABS(10-(X(1)+X(2)*5))
104 C2=ABS(12-(X(1)+X(2)*8))
105 C3=ABS(14-(X(1)+X(2)*9))
106 C4=ABS(16-(X(1)+X(2)*10))
```

```
107 C5=ABS(17-(X(1)+X(2)*12))
108 C6=ABS(18-(X(1)+X(2)*14))
109 C7=ABS(21-(X(1)+X(2)*16))
110 C=C1+C2+C3+C4+C5+C6+C7
120 IF C<M THEN 160
130 GO TO 170
160 A(1)=X(1),A(2)=X(2)
165 M=C
170 NEXT I
180 NEXT J
190 PRINT "THE SLOPE IS",A(2)
195 PRINT "THE INTERCEPT IS",A(1)
200 PRINT M,"IS THE TOTAL DEVIATION"
205 STOP
210 END


>RUN
14:58   DEC 19  RUNDCAA...
THE SLOPE IS   1.00000
THE INTERCEPT IS                 5.00000
 3.00000        IS THE TOTAL DEVIATION

>RUN
14:55   DEC 19  RUNDCAA...
THE SLOPE IS   1.00000
THE INTERCEPT IS                 4.99999
 3.00001        IS THE TOTAL DEVIATION

>RUN
14:57   DEC 19  RUNDCAA...
THE SLOPE IS   1.00000
THE INTERCEPT IS                 5.00000
 3.00000        IS THE TOTAL DEVIATION
```

21.

```
5  REM PART 1
10 REM AFTER CHAPTER 7
15 REM EXERCISE 21
```

```
20 PRINT "N","N FACTORIAL"
40 N=1
50 FOR I=1 TO 15
60 N=N*I
70 PRINT I,N
80 NEXT I
90 STOP
95 END
>RUN
14:33   DEC 19   RUNDCAA...
N               N FACTORIAL
 1                1
 2                2
 3                6
 4               24
 5              120
 6              720
 7             5040
 8            40320
 9           362880
10          3628800
11         39916800
12        479001600
13        6.22702E+09
14        8.71783E+10
15        1.30767E+12
```

_____PART TWO EXERCISES

2.

```
1     REM PART 2
2     REM AFTER CHAPTER 16
3     REM EXERCISE 2
5     DIM A(3),B(3),L(3),N(3),U(3),X(3)
7     F=2
10    X=1
12    M=1.0E30
```

```
14   FOR I2=1 TO 3
16   B(I2)=0,A(I2)=50,N(I2)=100
18   NEXT I2
20   FOR J=1 TO 6
21   FOR I=1 TO 700
24   FOR K=1 TO 3
30   IF A(K)-N(K)/F**J < B(K) THEN 50
40   GO TO 60
50   L(K)=B(K)
55   GO TO 65
60   L(K)=A(K)-N(K)/F**J
65   IF A(K)+N(K)/F**J > N(K) THEN 80
70   GO TO 90
80   U(K)=N(K)-L(K)
85   GO TO 100
90   U(K)=A(K)+N(K)/F**J-L(K)
100  X(K)=INT(L(K)+RND(X)*U(K))
102  NEXT K
103  C1=ABS(X(1)+2*X(2)+X(3)-36)
104  C2=ABS(X(1)+X(2)+X(3)-27)
105  C3=ABS(X(1)*X(2)+X(2)*X(3)-162)
106  C=C1+C2+C3
120  IF C< M THEN 160
130  GO TO 170
160  A(1)=X(1),A(2)=X(2),A(3)=X(3)
165  M=C
170  NEXT I
180  NEXT J
190  PRINT A(1),A(2),A(3)
200  PRINT M
210  STOP
215  END
```

```
>RUN
15:27    DEC 19   RUNXBAA...
 6              9              12
 0
```

3.

```
1    REM PART 2
2    REM AFTER CHAPTER 16
3    REM EXERCISE 3
4    REM THREE TRIES AND ONE SOLUTION
5    DIM A(3),B(3),L(3),N(3),U(3),X(3)
7    F=2
10   X=1
12   M=1.0E30
14   FOR I2=1 TO 3
16   B(I2)=-1000,A(I2)=0,N(I2)=1000
18   NEXT I2
20   FOR J=1 TO 11
21   FOR I=1 TO 700
24   FOR K=1 TO 3
30   IF A(K)-N(K)/F**J < B(K) THEN 50
40   GO TO 60
50   L(K)=B(K)
55   GO TO 65
60   L(K)=A(K)-N(K)/F**J
65   IF A(K)+N(K)/F**J > N(K) THEN 80
70   GO TO 90
80   U(K)=N(K)-L(K)
85   GO TO 100
90   U(K)=A(K)+N(K)/F**J-L(K)
100  X(K)=INT(L(K)+RND(X)*U(K))
102  NEXT K
103  C1=ABS(6*X(1)-3*X(2)+X(3)**2-18)
104  C2=ABS(9*X(1)+X(2)+X(3)-800)
106  C=C1+C2
120  IF C< M THEN 160
130  GO TO 170
160  A(1)=X(1),A(2)=X(2),A(3)=X(3)
165  M=C
170  NEXT I
180  NEXT J
190  PRINT A(1),A(2),A(3)
200  PRINT M
210  STOP
215  END
```

```
>RUN
15:34    DEC 19   RUNXBAA...
 72                159              -8
 2

     210 HALT
>RUN
15:35    DEC 19   RUNXBAA...
 33                468                 35
 1

     210 HALT
>RUN
15:36    DEC 19   RUNXBAA...
 16                701              -45
 0
```

Suggested Reading

American Journal of Mathematical and Management Sciences, vol. 1. Columbus, OH: *The American Sciences Press,* 1981.

Bajpai, A.C.; Calus, I.M; and Fairley, J.A. *Statistical Methods for Engineers and Scientists: A Student's Course Book.* New York: John Wiley, 1978.

Bajpai, A.C.; Pakes, H.W.; Clarke, R.J.; Doubleday, J.M.; and Stevens, T.J. *FORTRAN AND ALGOL: A Programmed Course for Students of Science and Technology.* New York: John Wiley, 1972.

Bajpai, A.C.; Calus, J.M.; and Fairley, J.A., eds. *Mathematics for Engineers and Scientists,* vol. 1. New York: John Wiley, 1973.

____. *Mathematics for Engineers and Scientists,* vol. 2. New York: John Wiley, 1973.

____. *Numerical Methods for Engineers and Scientists.* New York: John Wiley, 1977.

Bajpai, A.C.; Mustoe, L.R.; and Walker, D. *Specialist Techniques in Engineering Mathematics.* New York: John Wiley, 1980.

Beech, G. *FORTRAN IV in Chemistry—An Introduction to Computer-Assisted Methods.* New York: John Wiley, 1975.

Bellman, R. and Dreyfus, S. *Applied Dynamic Programming.* Princeton, N.J.: Princeton University Press, 1962.

Beltrami, Edward. *Models for Public Systems Analysis.* New York: Academic Press, 1977.

Bierman, H.; Bonini, C.; and Hausman, J. *Quantitative Analysis for Business Decisions.* 5th ed. Homewood, IL: Richard D. Irwin, 1981.

Carter, L.R. and Huzan, E.A. *Practical Approach to Computer Simulation in Business.* London: George Allen & Unwin Ltd., 1973.

Ceder, J. and Outcalt, D. *A Short Course in Calculus.* New York: Worth Publishers, 1968.

Charnes, A. and Cooper, W.W. *Management Models and Industrial Applications of Linear Programming.* New York: John Wiley, 1961.

Collatz, L. and Wetterling, W. *Optimization Problems.* New York: Springer-Verlag, 1975.

Conley, William. *Computer Optimization Techniques.* Princeton, N.J.: Petrocelli Books, 1980.

____. *Computer Optimization Techniques.* Rev. ed. Princeton, N.J.: Petrocelli Books, 1983.

____. *Optimization: A Simplified Approach.* Princeton, N.J.: Petrocelli Books, 1981.

____. *BASIC for Beginners.* Princeton, N.J.: Petrocelli Books, 1982.

Conley, William and Conley, William, Sr. "Computer Statistics Versus Calculus." In *COMPSTAT 80 Proceedings in Computational Statistics,* edited by M.M. Barritt and D. Wishart, pp. 355-361. Wurzburg, Vienna: Physica Verlag, 1980.

____. "A Fifty-Thousand Variable Nonlinear Problem." *COMPSTAT 1982 Short Communications Summaries of Posters,* edited by H. Caussinus, P. Ettinger, and J.R. Mathieu. Wurzburg, Vienna: Physica Verlag, 1982.

____. "Pricing a Product." *International Journal of Mathematical Education in Science and Technology* 12:63-67.

____. "Applications of Multi-Stage Monte Carlo Integer Programs." *International Journal of Mathematical Education in Science and Technology* 12:117-120.

____. "Solution of Polynomial Equations over the Complex Field." *International Journal of Mathematical Education in Science and Technology* 12:143-146.

____. "A Fifty-Variable Nonlinear Problem." *International Journal of Mathematical Education in Science and Technology* 12:265-269.

____. "Making a Prescription Drug." *International Journal of Mathematical Education in Science and Technology* 12:425-428.

____. "A 500-Variable Nonlinear Problem." *International Journal of Mathematical Education in Science and Technology* 12:609-617.

____. "A Ten Thousand Variable Nonlinear Problem." *International Journal of Mathematical Education in Science and Technology* 13:35-41.

____. "An Economic Order Quantity Problem." *International Journal of Mathematical Education in Science and Technology* 13:265-268.

____. "A Forty-Seven Equation Ninety-Variable Nonlinear System of Equations." *International Journal of Mathematical Education in Science and Technology* 13:311-315.

Cress, P; Dirksen, P.; and Graham, J. *FORTRAN IV with WATFOR & WATFIV.* Englewood Cliffs, N.J.: Prentice-Hall, 1970.

Dudewicz, E.J. and Ralley, T.G. *The Handbook of Random Number Generation and Testing with TESTRAND Computer Code.* Columbus, OH: American Science Press, 1981.

Eck, Roger, *Operations Research for Business.* Belmont, CA: Wadsworth, 1976.

Goldstein, L. and Loy, D. *Calculus and Its Applications.* Englewood Cliffs, N.J.: Prentice-Hall, 1981.

Greenburg, Michael. *Applied Linear Programming for the Socioeconomic and Environmental Sciences.* New York: Academic Press, 1978.

Hadley, G. *Nonlinear Programming.* Reading, MA: Addison-Wesley, 1964.

International Journal of Mathematical Education in Science and Technology 13. Issue on Mathematical Modeling (1982).

Hillier, F.S. and Lieberman, G.J. *Introduction to Operations Research.* San Francisco: Holden-Day, 1967.

Jaaskelainen, Veikko. *Linear Programming and Budgeting.* New York: Petrocelli/Charter, 1975.

Kemeny, John. *Man and the Computer.* New York: Scribners, 1972.

Kim, Chaiho. *Quantitative Analysis for Managerial Decisions.* Reading, MA: Addison-Wesley, 1976.

Lancaster, Kelvin. *Modern Economics Principles and Policy.* New York: Rand McNally, 1973.

Larson, Harold. *Introduction to Probability Theory and Statistical Inference.* New York: John Wiley, 1969.

Nickerson, C. and Nickerson, I. *Statistical Analysis for Decision Making.* Princeton, N.J.: Petrocelli Books, 1978.

Noble, Ben. "Applications of Undergraduate Mathematics in Engineering." *Mathematical Association of America*, 1967.

Sass, Joseph. *FORTRAN IV Programming and Applications.* San Francisco: Holden-Day, 1974.

Tinbergen, J. "Effects of the Computerization of Research". COMPSTAT 1978 Proceedings in *Computational Statistics,* pp. 20–28. Wurzburg, Vienna: Physica-Verlag, 1978.

Index